Into the
Fire

Into the Fire

Phyllis E. Leavitt, M.A.

Dedication

This book is dedicated to the Loving God who filled these pages, to our Mother Earth who holds life for us all, to the sacredness of our shared journey, and to the alleviation of the great human suffering that calls us urgently to all Return Together.

Contents

Acknowledgments

I would like to thank my dear husband Richard Jenkins, my fabulous editor Deborah Brown, my amazing children Eddie Konold, Isabella Konold and Daniel Konold, their spouses and partners- Katie Konold, Brandi Konold and Paul Rossano, and my dear friends Annie Lewis, Aggie Damron Garner, Charlotte Taft, Gwen Augusten and Liz Cervio. Thank you for your love, support, and guidance.

The Morning Prayer

I bow to myself
I bow to the Guru within
And the Guru without
Who are one and the same

I bow to all that is
All that was
And all that will be
With Supreme Surrender

I am not afraid
I step willingly
And with a pure heart
Out of the way

And I have faith in God
And in my own Soul
Who are one and the same.

Fire Prayer

I embody my Soul
In my eyes, in my words,
And in the vibration of my heart
I willingly walk
Through the Fires that are mine
And I am not burned
I am transformed
I find ultimate happiness and fulfillment
In being the truly faithful servant
Of all that my Soul
Has given me.

Introduction

O *pen your eyes. You can do it. The Fire that once burned you will now Redeem you. There is only God everywhere.*

Into the Fire is the second book in **The Road Home Series**. It picks up right where *A Light in the Darkness* leaves off. While you might be able to follow along without having read the first book, I highly recommend you read Book I before reading any other books in this series because Book I gives the complete background for everything that follows. There is a slow, steady building of experience and information that is much more easily followed if you start from the beginning.

It is impossible to summarize Book I and the unfolding wisdom that was shared with me in a few paragraphs. This wisdom emerged slowly as an ever-expanding beam of Divine light and love amidst personal experiences of great darkness. But in a nutshell, Book I tells the story of the pervasive darkness of my early life, my search for God, and the very few moments of transcendent awareness that pierced through the heavy cloud of pain and despair I lived in. It tells the story of how a Divine Voice began speaking to me in 1994 and went on speaking volumes for quite some time. I wrote down everything that was told to me. My purpose in writing **The Road Home Series** is to share that Love and Wisdom with you.

For anyone who decides to dive into this second book without reading Book I, there are some crucial topics you will want to be aware of. First, in the course of exploring the Darkness that pervaded my life, I uncovered memories of a past life in which I was burned at the stake as a witch. I apparently spoke out about a personal experience of Christ and was condemned as a heretic. This memory came with such agonizing clarity that it was undeniable. I was shocked to see that many people in my present life were central players in that past life. Thus, the door was opened to a new understanding not only of the road my own Soul has been traveling through lifetimes *with others*, but also to the *inter-relatedness* of all the parts we have played for each other over millennia. Specifics of the witch life continue to unfold in this second book, *Into the Fire.*

Secondly, I refer to a man I call T, as in Teacher. T was the person I was doing deep inner child and trauma work with at the time this Divine Presence came to me. T proved to be an amazing support and guide through the pain of all my memories — this life and past lives — and he was soulfully interested in all the messages I received. His trust and valuing of my process were unlike any affirmation I had ever received from anyone. And, as one of the Souls I have traveled with, he played a part in my own growth in other ways I could not have foreseen — all of which I honor, more than ever, as Teacher.

Thirdly, it will help you to know that much earlier in my life, at the ages of 20 and 21, I experienced a profound connection to the spirit of Mother Earth, who opened her doors and spoke to me during a magical summer I spent in the Mohave Desert, and then again on an equally magical afternoon in Boston Commons. I describe these experiences in *A Light in the Darkness,* as well as specific messages I received from Mother Earth after my work with the Divine Voice began in 1994.

Mother Earth has more to say in *Into the Fire*.

And lastly, I refer to a spiritual teacher named Swami Muktananda who I had met in NY in the early 80's. Although the short time I spent in his presence was very powerful for me, I did not like the ashram experience and I did not consider him my teacher. However, shortly after this Divine Voice began speaking to me in the early 90's, Muktananda, who had already passed away, suddenly appeared to me in meditation, and I share his messages to me in this present book.

I continued to sail a rocky sea. One wave lifted me up to the edge of Heaven and the next one took me under. But the Divine Presence gave me breath in uninhabitable places and without fail, shed exquisite light on what my particular Soul was doing in the difficult experiences of Phyllis Leavitt. That personal explanation always expanded into a panoramic view of what *all* our Souls are doing here in human form. I was told about the laws of ego — the great Sleep of Forgetting under which we operate — and how we can wake up to Soul Consciousness and be of Service to the entire human race and the planet Earth — each in our own unique way. Over time, I was given a new view of Jesus and the Christ energy, and detailed information about the chakras of humanity and the chakras of the Earth as receptors and transmitters of Divine energies. I was given prayers and meditations that anyone can work with as a guide on the journey Home.

And much much more.

If you have already read Book I, I am so happy to offer you a continuation of the profound Love and Wisdom that was so generously shared with me in this second book of **The Road Home Series,** *Into the Fire.*

Dear Reader

I have to tell you that as exciting as it was to actually complete and print Book I, on the eve of publication I found myself standing in an unexpected Fire. Well, it wasn't really unexpected. I knew that Fire was there, but I had been deliberately avoiding it. So, it wasn't until I turned around to face it that I realized how very *hot* it was. I'm talking about my present-day family. What would they think of all I had written? What new position of alienation would I find myself in now? Why was this always the next leg of the journey, the next Fire I had to walk through—speaking something that would surely make my life more difficult, perhaps more dangerous, and potentially hurt or offend people I love? But of course, I already knew the answer to that question. *Exactly this* is a big part of my journey, whether my personality likes it or not. And there is such a profound feeling that it is exactly *this Fire* that I came here to stand in and not be burned. It's just that it felt *so hot* as far as my present-day family was concerned.

On the other hand, I hoped that publishing the book could be a great relief. Okay—THIS is who I am, this is who I have always been, and this is my truth, for better or for worse... sigh...

It's one thing to write your heart out. It's quite another to have your writing read by others. And it's a completely different confrontation to have it be read by people who are actually part of your story and not necessarily portrayed in the most favorable light. I don't have a problem talking about some of the unattractive parts of my own personality — my powerlessness, anxiety and depression, my black sheep identity, my preoccupation with pain and darkness. Some people said it was courageous to write so vulnerably, but it really didn't take courage. I *had* to speak. Tell me, if your child was drowning and you had to jump into a raging river to save her, would you call it bravery if you made the leap? No, I don't think so. You do what you *have* to do. Well, a part of *me* was drowning and there really was no choice but to jump in.

Don't get me wrong. There *is* vulnerability, but it does not lie in revealing my personal trials — the vulnerability is about saying I heard messages from a Divine Source. Big flames there.

When the last edits of my manuscript were near completion and the book was about to go into print, I found myself sobbing with my husband and son Eddie over my birthday dinner in a fancy restaurant in Denver. Long and short of it — it finally broke through to consciousness that my family would very likely be hurt, disbelieving, or excruciatingly uncomfortable with my childhood memories and my past life recollections. I *did not* want to hurt anyone. The real point of my book wasn't even about childhood pain or past life trauma. The point of my book was the *incredible and unexpected good* that came out of it. The point was that each person's solitary journey from Darkness to Light can provide an opening into the Road we all walk together, the Road Home. The point was that there is a Divine Presence that is waiting to help us find our way.

But I didn't think my family would see it that way.

"The truth is always your friend." This has been a guiding principle in my life. It seemed I had no choice but to go down into the darkest "truths" of my own existence; they have yielded the greatest light for me. But it was hard to see how my family would receive my "truth" as any kind of "friend."

This was my Fire. I had to speak anyway.

I have to tell you that my now 99-year-old mother was the one I most feared hurting. She is in good health and very sound in mind, especially for someone her age, and I was quite sure she would read my book. Before it was actually in print, I wrote her a long letter, hoping to prepare her for the worst. I laid out my whole life in that letter—the extremes of anxiety, fear and loneliness I had suffered, the startling moments of Divine Love and, and finally the Voice of God and Soul that came to me in 1994.

I had no idea what this Fire would create. I just knew I had to walk through it. I knew and believed what my writing had told me—that we are all players on the same stage, that we play parts for each other on the Road of Karma and on the Road of Return, that none of us *is* the part we play—we are all Soul dressed in different costumes for the purpose of experience only, and for the purpose of Return ultimately. I know this and I believe this. But I still have to live it; I have to experience it over and over again, in my consciousness and in my heart. I have to experience it with the most difficult players in my play. I had to face my mother in the flesh with my truth, with my full story. And because there was nowhere else to go, I did. Writing her that letter broke the trance. *Miraculously* and *completely unexpectedly,* my attachment to the difficulty of the parts we have played for each other dropped away, and perhaps for the very first time, I knew I loved my mother beyond anything we had experienced or not experienced with each other in this life. And I wanted her to know that before she died.

My mother was surprisingly responsive. She called me right away after she received my letter. She told me she thought the letter was very courageous, that I was a very special person, though she just didn't live in the same world I did. She was lovely, generous and kind.

This level of exchange was a new experience for me with my mother. I was impressed and relieved, but I couldn't help thinking—Wait until she actually reads the book!!

Fast forward. When the book was finally in print, I sent copies to my family. Time moved for me in agonizing slow motion. With every day that went by, I felt the white heat of a slow burn in my heart. Tears poured out of me in embarrassing places. I said a mantra every day, many times a day—"I willingly walk through the Fires that are mine and I am not burned. I am transformed." If Soul wanted me to burn off some big chunk of ego in this Fire, I would say yes.

Weeks went by. I've done it now, I thought. I'm one of those people whose family doesn't speak to them. How did I get here? It reminded me of the surreal feelings I had after I left my ex-husband, Bill. I would wake up in the morning and feel myself floating over my life, unable to find a place to land, the landscape suddenly unfamiliar and shockingly barren. It wasn't *quite* the same now. I have a landing spot today and my life is anything but barren, but even so, something essential was achingly out of alignment, like a bone that has popped out of joint and you can't get it back into place.

And then my mother called. She was reading the book and she liked it! She told me she looked forward to reading more. She acknowledged that it didn't portray her very positively…

I have to stop right there. *She acknowledged that it didn't make her look all that good and she was still open to the book and to me…* She blew me away! I was so impressed, so grateful. And then

I thought, Okay, wait until she reads about the past lives…gasp…

But she called me again when she finished it, and she talked about all the parts of the book she loved. She **did not** believe in past lives, she said. Fine, that's totally okay. And then she went on to say, "Well, I may have killed you in a past life, but I gave you life in this one!" And you know what, *she did*. We *both* asked for a chance to redo it, and in the nick of time we got it.

I went to visit my mother a few months later. The trance was truly broken, the spell of lifetimes lifted. *Nothing* stood in the way of our having some very sweet moments together — no particular conversation, but the embraces we shared were real. I sought them out as much as she did. "We're friends," she said as I was leaving, "We love each other." Yes. And I cried and cried when I got home for all the years that had gone by without that tenderness, for all that we had not been able to be for one another, for all that *I* had not been able to give *her*.

Remember I told you that as a child I used to lie in bed at night terrified that our house would burn down and I would have no way to escape my second-floor bedroom? Well, that old house finally did burn down, and I didn't die after all.

I've come back for you, my little witch self. I've come back for you. You will not die this way again… but so much easier said than done.

***

There is a pattern that is very old in your spirit's path of descent and ascent that has to do with living your truth in secrecy and facing the fear of death and destruction if you were found out or if you spoke out. You are asked to speak out once again, for many reasons. Many purposes come together through your voice, and now you see the Serpent comes out of your mouth and his eyes are wide open and he speaks for you and through you as you allow it. With your voice, you redeem the Scream. Be as present to the voice as it is possible for you to be. Feel your Teacher in the center of your heart. Feel Teacher climb into your throat and fill your mouth and exit in the form of the Serpent. See your voice as an instrument and use it to be very present inside your Temple. Stay inside your Temple. The voice you speak will Teach you. You are asked to speak. This writing is one level. It is your Teacher on paper. There are other Teachers. Inside your Temple, you are to bow down to them all. Though you do not yet know them, they will make themselves known to you. The Serpent will uncoil inside you and you are not allowed to stop it.

How to Read This Book

There are three "voices" speaking in this book:

Present Day Narrative: Plain text

Divine Voice (from 1995-1996): *Italicized text*

Journaling Voice (from 1995 to 1996): Indented text called out as below

> I don't know what this means, but I saw an image of a great Pearl opening up and all the myriad forms and wonders of the Earth spilled out for me to see. The Earth was this great Pearl inverted so that everything not visible on the inside became visible on the outside. He said that the intrinsic, essential energy form of the Earth is Pearl energy.

Definitions
In the back of the book there is a list of definitions of the terms that are central to the concepts that emerge in the communication from the Divine Voice that spoke to me.

~ *Phyllis*

Chapter 1

The Serpent

T he house is silent and empty. I light a stick of incense and a candle and put a chanting tape into the stereo. A solitary worshiper at her lonely altar. No words of prayer on my lips, only a muted supplication that has been there for as long as I can remember... Help me...

T and his partner have just left—I did a reading for them, and just moments ago I was in a space of golden light, seamlessly connected to other realms and other times. They put on their coats and whisked themselves away into the forbidden world of coupledom, already nicely dressed for their next event. My body is still sitting on my couch in my living room, clean and neat and still, but I have fallen over the edge of the earth, and I topple headlong and backwards into a cosmic void I know so well. A loneliness like death is everywhere....

Help me...

I press Play. I close my eyes and open my throat. I let my voice come out and allow it to be swallowed up in the ocean of voices singing with me. I let the chorus in and slowly my voice becomes stronger. My whole life is in my throat. There is nowhere else for it to go... Help me...

Suddenly I see a Serpent.

He is standing very rigid and straight with his head up at the top of my head, his mouth wide, and a huge pink lotus opening out from his mouth. Golden light vibrates again in the center of my forehead. And then a huge, intensely blue burst of light fills my head like an enormous blue circle exploding into hundreds of deep blue stars.

Hell becomes heaven once again.

Muktananda appears holding a large staff and the end of the staff is brilliant with white gold light that becomes more and more brilliant and bigger and bigger until the top of the staff goes into the top of my head. The Serpent is coiled up the whole length of the staff, his mouth wide open, and he is chanting with me. Muktananda tells me to stop chanting and just listen, and I feel him very big, as if in person, standing over me, walking back and forth in front of me. He puts his thumb on my forehead and keeps putting it there again and again. When he finally takes it away, there are ashes on my forehead where he touched me. I know that the ashes are a symbol of death, that something in me is burned, that the ashes he put on my forehead are what is left and that it is very holy. I hear, *You wear your death as a symbol of the life that emerges from the ashes.* I call in all past life parts of myself to be with me while he paces around me like a huge lion, and I listen.

And then Muktananda sits in the lotus position at the base of my spine. I understand that I am the Way, and that I am to bow down to the Temple of myself. That Muktananda coming to sit inside me is to show me that God dwells in each of us, and the more we know this, the more we act with this knowledge in mind, the more it will become impossible to hurt ourselves or hate ourselves or belittle ourselves. He says, *Why not see me inside you everywhere, in relation to everything?* And so I fight the fear of being presumptuous and I say to myself —you are a Divine being. You are not a leper.

***

And so, another new chapter opened, though as always, I could not have understood the significance at the time. The Divine Voice simply said —

This is a gift that is being given wholeheartedly, not conditionally, for the very reason of helping you overcome your tremendous self-judgment — not if you are good enough or in the right state or pure enough. For the very reason of helping you understand that your outward appearance is not what God looks at. You see it is only self-judgment that makes you deny what is given.

The next day I went to a Satsang, a gathering of Muktananda devotees who met weekly in someone's living room to mediate and chant. I took my place crossed legged on the floor, hoping for invisibility, self-conscious even in that setting where no one would be focused on me at all.

> During the chant, I seemed to be particularly disconnected from my body. Usually I sway gently with the music, but this time I was barely moving. But toward the end, Muktananda came inside me once again, to sing with me and through me. Suddenly I felt a very strong physical sensation like electricity, like a snake slithering up my spine in a very exotic and dance-like way. And my body danced with it of its own accord.
>
> Then just as suddenly I saw the vision of a noose and a past life memory exploded through to consciousness.
>
> I am being hanged. I am a young man, a bit stocky. I am a perpetrator of some kind, or they think I am. A crime involving sex. Derision all around me. Someone kicks away what I am standing on. And right there in the Satsang, a sharp pain shoots across the sole of my foot, exactly as I must have felt it in that life... My neck jerks back.

Then I left that scene and an incredibly powerful vision of a noose made of two Serpents with a body hanging suspended from them appeared before me. The Serpents were coiled around the neck and they were extended high above the head in a way that looked almost beautiful, so graceful, as if it were a painting from an ancient Tarot card. In that moment… Still sitting there in the Satsang, the sharp pain in my foot was *undeniable!*

My foot is still a little bit sore this morning. I have a hard time letting this in, but my body has its own reality. I have a voice that wants to come in so badly that says that I am getting so far out there that even if I don't feel like a crazy person, I will be perceived as one. I'm having a *physical* past life memory? I'm so afraid I am going out on a limb that will be sawed off and there will be no way back for me, no way back to some ordinary "safe" reality, a reality that was never safe for me anyway. Then my Divine Voices said—

*Many sense perceptions **that are beyond the five senses** will open up to you along this road. The vision of the two Serpents forming a noose is a symbol of exactly where you are. The power of the Serpents can kill you or it can be the doorway to the other side. You can hang yourself with what you know and what you see or you can hang your old view of life and of yourself. The Serpents in your vision come to tell you that you can now go back to that lifetime and all lifetimes and **die consciously**. Die to what was. Die to everything that keeps you in the personal, die to all sex that is bound to aggression. Die to fear, die to craziness. The only noose worth fearing is the one you tie around your own neck. When the Serpents take you by the throat, you are being asked to die to everything you thought you knew.*

That is why the symbol you saw is beautiful rather than grotesque or terrifying.

The difficulty of believing myself is enormous. But there is just too much at this point that is beyond doubt. And yet I am frightened regardless.

Indeed, the Serpent was waking me up from deep sleep. No, he was not wakening me into some hoped-for state of pure bliss. This Serpent was waking me up to lifetimes of conditioning that had blanketed my vision, waking me up to all that concealed the God within. This Serpent brought seeming death as the portal to life.

***

I was given glimpses of other previous lives, though none of those memories were as complete as the witch lifetime. In many of the lives I was shown, I was accused of heresy and killed for what I had spoken about my beliefs. In each lifetime, I was taken directly to the moment of death and the state I was in when I died—most often fear, confusion, self-doubt, self-blame, and disconnection from the faith I had experienced in that life. In one life, I saw myself as a woman killed in the Inquisition, and in another I was a monk locked in a cell for the rest of his life for speaking about a spiritual experience. These were lives, like the witch life, in which I naively thought my faith would be pleasing to the church. In yet another life, I saw myself as a young housemaid murdered for telling that she had been raped by the owner of the house, and in a totally different life I saw myself as the young man mentioned above who was accused of rape and hanged. I saw myself as a Native American man who had an intense connection to the natural world, killed senselessly by white men. And in the last life I was shown, I was a seven-year-old Jewish girl who died in the Holocaust.

I was also shown two much earlier lives. In one, I was a young woman who appeared to be part of a very early group of Native Americans in North America. Her name was Talking Flower and she lived a short life in which she literally had a talking relationship with the plants. She could communicate with the natural world as easily as she could communicate with people. Talking Flower died young but she appeared to have no trauma and her consciousness in that lifetime felt peaceful and complete. And then, ages and ages before that life, I saw myself as a prehistoric humanoid type male creature who, as he lay dying in a cave, was trying to make sounds that would communicate his pain to others. He was experiencing the very beginning of human language. It was the oddest past-life memory. I could feel myself inside his minimally developed brain searching to express a feeling.

The message to me was to die all those deaths consciously, and especially to die again to all that had killed me in the past. What did this mean? I was shown that the state of consciousness we were in when we died in previous lives, along with the beliefs we held about ourselves and others, follow us into future lives in exactly the same way that unresolved issues from our present-day childhoods follow us into present-day adulthood.

In psychotherapy, it is the current lifetime conditioning that is seen as problematic and the work is to "Undo" its negative impact. That is all I could conceive of and all I had hoped for when I originally started working with T in 1993. Then, when the Divine Voice began speaking to me, I saw that present-day issues and beliefs are representative of a much larger pattern our Souls have been playing out through the whole course of our incarnations, and that this is true for us all.

In psychotherapy, we re-work early negative experiences to create emotional healing, so that our healthy *adult selves* can take over and direct our lives in more mature, fulfilling and responsible ways. On another round of that same spiral, my Divine Voice was telling me that we can rework all the conditioning of *ego consciousness* accumulated over lifetimes so that our *Souls* can take over the direction of our lives, return us to Divine Love, and express that Divine Love in the world. The unresolved energies of past lives are just as present in our psyches as the energies and issues of our present life. In fact, they are the same energies.

Putting all those energies back into the Fire and burning consciously means burning away all the ego illusions and beliefs that still haunt us and keep the light of Soul from shining through. For me that meant burning away the false belief that my truth would surely kill me, that I was doomed to eternal solitude, and much more.

Die consciously. Easier said than done... The ashes Muktananda put on my forehead and the image of the Serpent noose, beautiful as those images were, still inspired fear. I wasn't asking *to die* to anything. I was asking *to LIVE!* And yet the two became one. Dying consciously, dying to my old view of life, seemed to be the access to new life in Soul.

I understood that the healing energies and levels of Soul consciousness we have experienced in past lives are carried over into our present existence. Talking Flower was not a part that I needed to die to. She carried a pure piece of Soul consciousness and she, too, was influencing my journey.

I felt her presence many times during these years of intense writing between 1995 and 1998. I believe it was her energy that opened up the profound experiences I had in the Mohave Desert, Boston Commons, at the stream in Tesuque, and that would make possible conversations with other aspects of Mother Earth that were to come. And in a way I may never quite understand or be able to describe, the Divine Voice that fills these pages does not feel entirely new either. The messages it brings are very present day, but the Voice and the place from which these messages arise, are also a part of my "history."

All this is clear now, but in those early days of the writing, the emotions still attached to my current childhood, combined with the terror pushing through from past lives, made the prospect of successfully dying to anything nearly inconceivable. Nevertheless, the journey continued without a pause. There was no relief back then in 1995, nor do I think I particularly wanted any. The train was moving so fast, I just held on the best I could. I continued to suffer bouts of anxiety interrupted by bursts of great Light. I wasn't finished, by any means, exploring the intense Darkness that brought me to Them in the first place.

There is much dark energy still surrounding your light. Know that the Darkness is there. Know that every time you feel the Love of God pouring in over you, the Darkness of old patterns and beliefs will be further revealed.

This was exactly my experience, even before They came. Every experience of Divine connection plunged me into a new experience of Darkness. I thought it was a fatal flaw that those moments of Divine Love didn't seem to heal me. In all the years I tried to follow spiritual paths, I had never heard that Light *continuously* reveals more about the Darkness that binds us, that we do not necessarily have one huge breakthrough catharsis and then we are free. I was still learning that the Darkness is exactly what we came to work with if we are going to make the journey Home at all. At least, that is how it has been for me.

*God's love is Divine Light in the Darkness of the Horizontal Plane. It may feel that the Darkness lies in ambush waiting to burn you or hang you. But this Darkness is only real on the Horizontal Plane. This Darkness is the Shadow of the Holy Ghost that you have internalized for centuries and believed was a part of you. That is all it is for anyone. The Shadow of the Holy Ghost is **projected ego energy** which is internalized, believed, and acted out in the world of ego consciousness, which then further tightens and strengthens* *the web of ego energies in which human beings form and solidify their beliefs about themselves and determine what strategies they will use to survive.*

*Your task is to **die consciously** to all previous lives, to "Undo" and give back all projected ego energies – endless judgments, comparisons, ego expectations – taken on and internalized over the course of your incarnations. Your task is to "Undo" the hold that the laws of ego consciousness have on your psyche. **Dying consciously does not mean detaching, not caring, or leaving this world. It means being right here at "A" and facing, digesting and transforming all ego energies coming from within and projected from without.***

Perhaps the recognition that I had lifetimes of projections to Undo might have felt overwhelming, but in fact it was a relief. It made sense – the constriction in my throat, the belief that my truth would be my undoing – it all made a larger sense. I wasn't crazy; I was dealing with *lifetimes* of Darkness. And it was a relief, too, to see a pattern emerging. The unresolved energies from other lifetimes were intricately connected both to the issues of my present life and to the *people* in my present life! And, as a counterpoint, I had resources from other lives to draw on. Whatever energies I been able to Redeem in past lives also traveled with me, and the Souls of those sharing that part of my journey were surely with me, too. The dense web of ego was beginning to be unraveled. I had a new understanding of my own human nature that was inconceivable only a few months before. AND, I was still very much living in that whirlwind of projection. I understood it better, but I was certainly not free of it.

*Do you see now why you needed to go back to the witch lifetime and stand in the Fire and give back all the Darkness to the people who projected it onto you? **You cannot give back the Darkness fully and truly unless you understand that it is not an intrinsic part of you. It is not.** It is not an intrinsic part of anyone. As* *long as you are willing to absorb the Darkness for any reason, you stay in ego consciousness. In Reality, you don't actually "give" Darkness to anyone. More accurately, when you do not absorb projected ego energies, those from whom it issued forth are left with those energies to deal with themselves. When you no longer absorb these projections, your fear will vanish, your doubt will vanish, your separateness will vanish. Just remember what a shadow is. It is not an entity in and of itself. It is the absence of light. It is created by something blocking the path of light. When you remove the block, there is no more shadow. The block is the ego beliefs you have absorbed from lifetimes of experience on the Horizontal Plane and they are NOT TRUE.*

I did not know how to work with projections back then. That understanding would unfold as the dialogue with the Divine Voice continued. But I was learning that true protection lies in Undoing all the ways I still *believed* those projections of judgment I had absorbed.

***

Help continued to flood in on me from all angles. I wrote and wrote. Mother Earth spoke to me again. Muktananda and the Serpent came to me in chanting and meditation, always appearing as vividly as if they were there in the flesh. Every difficult life experience seemed to be the perfect entry into what my Divine Voice came to teach me next. And the information came *so* fast. Perhaps it was intended that I get it all down quickly, as if there was only so much time for me to record a huge body of information. It did not seem to matter that I could not possibly incorporate it all into my life that quickly. At the same time, I was not just an observer or a scribe. The meanings, implications and the level of consciousness from which the writing came, were all etched directly into my brain and my heart in the transmission. But the ordinary life emotions that overcame me much of the time made it very difficult to apply what I heard for more than a few moments at a time.

Some people walk on coals as a spiritual practice, as an initiatory trial. Others meditate for hours or chop wood and carry water, walk barefoot and penniless through the desert, or renounce all earthly delights. My initiation was walking the tightrope of my own sanity over an inferno of presumption, heresy, and fiery shrieks of "Who do you think you are?" crackling wildly behind my eyeballs. Nevertheless, my internal reality was becoming more real than anything tangible outside me. The idea of Reality altogether was morphing into a visually stunning, internal, heart-pounding vibration.

Thankfully, I had T. My sessions with him at that time were my lifeline to sanity. He seemed to recognize all the symbols, feel the energies, and honor the wisdom I was receiving. In the small but extraordinary world T and I inhabited together, I was not crazy.

Perhaps ancient symbols are not really mythical at all. I understand now that Serpent Power is the energy that put the human race into its original Sleep of Forgetting, and that Serpent Power is also of the energy that wakes us up to the Road of Return. No wonder it is the Serpent who plays such a central role in the story of Adam and Eve, who was said to have provided the temptation that got us cast out of Eden and set man and woman apart from each other and from God. I understand now that the Serpent in that pivotal story symbolizes our falling into the Sleep of Forgetting. Perhaps that is the real Fall.

The Serpent that came to me held the power of our Waking Up.

Chapter 2

The Plant World Speaks

My daughter had moved to California and her addiction was spinning out of control beyond my reach. My youngest child, Daniel, was just hitting adolescence and I didn't think I had one more ounce of energy to deal with a teenager. I joked about just skipping the next four years and resuming life at his graduation, but it wasn't entirely a joke. And Eddie, my oldest, who left for a three-month wilderness experience in Patagonia as a boy, returned a man. Although he had spent much of his teenage years lost in an aimless, pot-filled fog, he didn't have to wait until his forties to hear the call of his Soul. He burned off that low-lying cloud of unconsciousness by the time he was twenty.

An acquaintance saw us walking up a hill one day shortly after he returned from South America, the sun shining through his blond hair. She later asked me who I was walking with because it looked like I was walking with an angel. I said that's my son, and he is an angel. But even his light didn't pierce my darkness. And although my most incredible Divine Presence truly did everything imaginable to light up my flickering Soul, Phyllis herself was beyond depleted. My pain and my loss felt like a burden no one else could understand or tolerate, no one but T, who of course I paid to help me inch my way through the Wilderness. But thankfully, T was genuinely inspired by my journey and the best fellow traveler I could have asked for at that time.

Otherwise, comfort in the world of people was beyond my reach. Then Mother Earth stepped in again and opened up my vision when I needed her the most. Surely Talking Flower was there with me, too. The plant world spoke. I don't know that I can ever convey how blessed I was that these extraordinary experiences came to me regardless of how lost and powerless I felt—evidence, I believe, that we are *all* truly loved by God just as we are.

> Not having a great day. Don't understand how to apply what You said. It's all so confusing and painful— my attachment to other people, to what they think and feel about me and—what I think and feel about them and myself. I wish I *had* a little detachment. Digesting it all seems so difficult. Everywhere I go I still feel like an alien, can't find a comfortable place to be inside my own skin. Dying to it is beyond me. I just want to be with the plant world, with my little garden friends. The vine covering the wall of my back yard says—

Don't be sad, little mother, we are with you. Come and be with us. Your body is tired and you don't feel well. Come and rest in us. When the body aches or is tired, focus on the body. Look how much energy we expend on our bodies. We live and breathe to create our flowers and our fruit and the seeds to regenerate ourselves. We love being in our bodies, no matter if we are thistles, goat-heads, orchids, mangos or oak trees. We love our bodies without question and unconditionally. We are in touch, in our living waking consciousness, with the great cycles of birth and death and rebirth over eons of creation and contraction. We actually live in that reality and we feel intense joy in that reality just as we take great joy in every seed that sprouts, every flower that opens, every fruit that ripens and, yes, every fruit that is eaten. We take unending joy in what we are and what purposes we serve.

We, the plant world, have an unbelievably harmonizing effect on the planet. This is true on all levels—physical, emotional and spiritual.

We harmonize the world. You human beings are doing a good job of counteracting our effect. This is one of the real dangers to the planet right now. When the rain forests are destroyed, it is not just oxygen production or topsoil conservation or animal and plant species that are negatively affected. It is also the emotional and spiritual life of every manifest form that is affected. Our harmonizing effect on all levels is diminished.

Why do you think we ask you to breathe with us? This is not just a figure of speech. It is literally what is needed for all of us right now. You can literally breathe in our harmonizing energy. This is a true form of meditation. Feel the difference between an office building with plants and one without plants. So, we are saying to you, little mother, when you don't feel as connected as you would like to be, we are here in the flesh as your friends. We offer you at every moment everything we have to give. We offer you entrance. Do you see that we share a mutual love for each other? Never forget how much we love you, how much we love all human beings and all life on this planet. Why do you think we call to you so loudly? We love it when you talk to us and take joy in us. Just like you, we, too, are not intended to live and breathe in an isolated position in the world.

We are telling you, little mother, that there is nothing greater than loving the flesh of your own body, the fruit and the seed of your own existence. Not only is there nothing greater, THERE IS NOTHING ELSE. Every time you mistakenly think there is something missing from your life, think of us in our divine simplicity. We do nothing but worship God and serve the planet day in and day out. We exist, live, breathe, send out our vibrations and receive messages from every aspect of existence – AS A UNIT, AS ONE. We exist on a whole different level than human beings. We have no issues of our own. But we call to you en masse to think about what you are doing.

Don't be sad because you haven't found a perfect fit with your fellow human beings. There is not a lot for you to fit in with as yet. We are not saying to turn your back on humanity either. You have not yet found your "place," as it were, but be like us. See yourself as an individual part but at the same time as united with the human race.

Breathe with them. Breathe into them as we do with you. But do not for one more moment of your existence accept and judge yourself by values that have nothing whatsoever to do with Reality. The main difference of this lifetime for you, dear one, is that **this time, if you choose, you can leave the value system of separateness.** *But you see, don't you, that you cannot leave your brothers and sisters of the human race to do this, for you still see yourself as separate from them. This you must heal. You have always known this.*

It is time for you to love your body as we love ours. You are all seeds that have sprouted on this Earth from the same Divine tree, and as such, you are supremely lovable and supremely loved. It is time to see yourself and all others through these eyes. Look, we are all the same color — green. The sun works on chlorophyll the same way in all of us and we are many different shades of green together. Look what you do to each other with the slight variations in your skin color. Imagine if the plant world operated on such premises, on such fears.

Your society's values around body and image and appearance are extremely destructive and very sad. We cry for it. Hear this: We cry for how separate you believe yourselves to be. We cry for how you use sex, the ability given by God to produce seed and fruit and to feel joy in that process — we cry for how you use it as a weapon and as a judgment of self and as an escape from the rest of the turmoil you have created. We cry for what you, as a race, are now doing to your own seed and your own fruit.

Love your body now. Take care of your body now. For there is a whole world of secrets contained in your body that is not accessible to you any other way. You want to know how to apply what We are saying. Loving your body is the first step. Without this first step there is nothing else to learn. You already love your children, the fruit of your seed. Love their father also. Love what was possible through him. He will find his way in his own time.

Never fear asking entrance into our world. We are so close, you haven't even begun to imagine how close. We, too, will never leave you. We welcome you with all our heart. Because you see, we are all one. That's all we have ever been trying to say. See yourself through new eyes. Consciously shed your old vision like a dry and useless skin. Slide out of it and sit with us in the sun.

How to convey to you the overwhelming awe I felt at receiving messages so timeless and universally loving from the vine in my backyard? The plant world spoke to me that day as effortlessly as I might have spoken to a neighbor, and it wrapped me in a sheath of green wisdom beyond anything an ordinary conversation could have approached. This was the world I imagine Talking Flower inhabited daily in her short but ecstatic life where all was truly One.

And I was Talking Flower, too. In a way I cannot explain, she returned to me through this message from the plant world and reminded me of a part of who I am — who we all are. I could feel that profound green wisdom return to me, calling to me from somewhere deep beneath the lifetimes of shame about my body I still carried. But the prospect of loving my body at that time was as far-fetched as flying. I did not love my body. I ran from it, from my image in the mirror, from the constant comparison to more beautiful women, from the thought of exposure to men, and from the relentless pain and anxiety my body housed and unleashed at the tiniest opening.

So, I cannot repeat the wisdom of the plant world to myself often enough, even today — to love my own body as much as I love this Mother Earth, as a part of Mother Earth.

What would our world be like if we were all taught from birth to love the bodies we are born into — no sin, no shame, no judgment, no comparison — nothing but love, acceptance, honoring, and gratitude — and if we were taught to love the bodies that *everyone* is born into? A major projection of negative ego energies would be lifted like a dark veil from our vision of ourselves.

We do not have the feelings you do. We are not afraid to grow, we are not afraid of being chopped down. We don't like that but we are not afraid. We do not fear that the wall will crumble suddenly and we will fall. We just grow and grow, in our time and in our season. **Live in your immortality now, as we do.** *The power of God to create life and sustain life and transform life is where your immortality lies. If you understand that, if you live and breathe that, you can write any book you want, build any structure you want, create any beauty, love anything and anyone, and it will be in God's name. Otherwise it is more grist for the mill of your evolution and there is no blame.*

Chapter 3

Supreme Surrender

C hanting seemed to be my biggest solace outside my sessions with T. Looking back, it seems obvious that chanting gave me a way to open my throat in safety and connect with others, even if it was most often only with their recorded voices. Though I sometimes felt insane chanting alone in my office in a language I didn't even understand, in a strange way, I also felt sung to, like Soul was singing me a lullaby from another realm.

> On Monday night I chanted again. I couldn't get myself into it, so I prayed to Muktananda to help me and right away he said, *Let me come inside you.* He showed me how to stay centered in my breathing and he came into me to chant with me. He told me,

*Breathe me inside of you. Don't look at my picture and see me as separate from you. When you breathe me inside you we are one. You can breathe the whole world into you in this way. How can you breathe something into you if you are afraid of it? This is why you must work with fear, anger, doubt and judgment. The sound of the chant is a **connecting** vibration. When you chant, you connect to everything through the sound. Be in the sound in that way. This is Real.*

This is the Real World you enter in this way. I say that when you connect to God, you enter God's world, and that is the world of Omniscience and Omnipotence and Divine Love. You have no idea how many realms can open for you in this world. Breathe with **all** *things — this is the doorway.*

Later: I feel You in my heart and throat. Last night I went to Satsang and it felt really good to be there. We chanted Mere Baba and I focused as much as I could on breathing in Muktananda and giving my life to the Guru. He insisted that I do not see him as outside me at all. So, every time I even visualized his face, he said, *No, not that way,* and then again he moved inside me.

He showed me a Circle that was just him and me and he said this is a Soul Circle, the Circle of a Soul and the Guru and then he showed me how there is a long line of these Circles — the Circle of Muktananda and his Guru and all the Souls and their Gurus before that — and that this line of Soul Circles goes all the way back to God. Then he showed me a Circle with me and himself and God in it and he said this is another view of the Holy Trinity, or the Three in the One — Soul, Guru, and God. He said that the Guru and the Holy Ghost can also be seen as one, to see the whole world around me as my Teacher.

Again, he chanted with me and his mouth merged with mine and at the same time the Serpent's mouth also merged with mine, so there were our three mouths chanting together. Then I saw a vivid image of a Serpent coming straight out of my heart like a lily growing up out of the water, and I don't have any idea what it meant, but the image was very powerful.

When I allowed myself to chant with Muktananda inside me, my voice became much stronger and there was the feeling that I need to be in the world this way, with a sense of the presence and power of Teacher inside me, that this is a way of being, not just a practice.

Over and over Muktananda insisted on being inside me and then he said, *I am really always inside you but you don't see me. Open your Third Eye.* And at that moment I saw a light eye in the middle of my forehead. He told me to see him, feel him, and know him as inside me everywhere, not just in chanting and meditation.

Then Muktananda said: **Supreme Surrender to the Guru is Surrender to WHAT IS.**

I could not have known it then, but this one statement was to become the most important statement I would ever hear. **Supreme Surrender is Surrender to What Is.** Hadn't I spent a lifetime resisting What Is, judging What Is, trying to be anything other than what I believed myself to be, and believing that other people and the world itself should be different as well? Weren't we supposed to try to be better, more, different? This view of Surrender would unfold in exquisite detail over the next two years, and it was unlike any description of Surrender I had ever heard.

***

You remember a long time ago when you saw the videotape of a murder on the news. You remember how you asked God to be of service. We want to talk about Service from Our point of view. There are deeds that are considered "good" in the world. There are acts of kindness like giving money to the poor and rescuing a stray animal or stopping to help someone in an accident, returning something you borrowed and saving a piece of cake for someone else. There are other acts of service like cleaning up the environment, lobbying against child abuse or championing minority rights. These "good deeds" are not always "good" on an energy level. Good, of course, is an inadequate and very relative word. If a person works avidly to clean up the environment but sends out hate to the polluters of the world, the value of the deed is what? If a person gives everything to others and this giving comes from a place of poor valuing of self, the value of the giving is what? If a "good deed" is done as a way to barter for the love of others or the love of God, what exactly is the value of the deed? You get the point.

*The Service We talk about is not really about deeds. It is about Service to God, not to religion or religious dogma, but Service to God and Soul within. This is not exactly the same as service to mankind, **though one necessarily brings the other**. It is about Faith in the power of God in your life. Have the Faith to go where you are directed to go from within—with or without whatever you might consider reassurance from the outside. **Service, Phyllis, is a state of being. It is not in essence an action, although it will inevitably manifest as action in some form as long as you are in body. Every state of Being manifests in some form, but see that manifestation as a lawful outgrowth of the place in consciousness from which it arises. On the Road Home, as you Surrender ego to the Love and Wisdom inherent in your own Soul, you will begin to understand exactly how your Soul wishes to Serve the highest good of all. You will learn why your Soul incarnated into the form that is you and how you are the exact vehicle needed for Soul to participate in the evolution of human conscious- ness and Return for the human race.***

***This is Supreme Surrender to the Guru within.** You begin with Surrender to What Is, to exactly who you are, the energies you carry, and the energies you encounter. We are not talking about Surrender to a person but to the Principle of Teacher inside and outside. And you cannot fully learn from What Is unless you Surrender to What Is. This is the doorway and the Map and the Road of Return. You ask entrance into this every time you are with yourself and others exactly as you are, rather than chafing under the weight of what you imagine you or others should be. You ask entrance into this every time you breathe with Muktananda, every time you chant, and every time you breathe with the particular deities that present themselves to you. Every time you write with Us, you ask entrance into the Real world. **Walk through this Fire of Faith**. There is nowhere else to walk.*

As We have told you before, everyone has his own Guru. But even if you have a Master in the flesh, the principle is the same. A true guru guides you to the Master in your own heart and Soul. And for many, the Guru principle speaks solely through events: a crucial relationship, a certain type of loss, a natural catastrophe or a supreme success — or both, or all.

Chapter 4

Evolution: Sand and Pearls

I had many Teachers. One of my biggest teachers was relentless anxiety. Bowing to it, Surrendering, was an ongoing challenge. But it was also a great gift; it provided the opening for an understanding of our evolutionary process.

Today I woke up very early and was in a panic again. I did not even try to figure out why or what it is about because it is always about insecurity and loneliness. I just said the mantra over and over and tried to feel Muktananda within me. Even though there were no dramatic results, I stayed with it and after a very long time I did start to feel a little better. Being with What Is right now feels like standing in an enormous Fire. There is a part of me that wants to ask what is the point of all these incredible experiences I have if I just continue to battle panic over and over again? What does Surrender mean in the face of this intolerable feeling? But I know that is the negative part of me that has always believed that I am bad and hopeless because I have so much pain. The more I can see pain as the raw material of my evolution, as Soul calling me Home, as You have said, the more I know I will begin to walk through my Fires and be in alignment with You. I realize that walking through one's Fires means walking through them consciously. I have never done this before. I have kind of held on for dear life until each crisis passed and though

I know I have tried my best at times to stay present and accept deeply whatever was happening, I never had a true direction that was clear to me or that I was able to sustain.

Chanted for a little while last night. I had a hard time focusing but something interesting happened. My effort now is to breathe with the Guru inside me and chant with the Guru. Muktananda told me to focus my energy and attention on the sound of the words in the chant and breathe in the sound. He told me that I must begin to look at myself as a divine being. He reminded me of the vision I had of Buddha with his arms over his head in the position of the roof of a temple and he said I must see my whole self as a temple of God and no part of myself as not that.

Then at some point, Muktananda told me to direct the energy to the middle of my forehead and as I did that, I saw that in my forehead was a Pearl, that the energy form or symbol of the Third Eye is the Pearl. Then I saw the Serpent standing very tall and erect with the Pearl in its mouth, holding it very delicately in its fangs, as if it were the most fragile egg, and the Serpent was looking straight at me. Muktananda told me that the Earth, in some way that we human beings cannot yet conceptualize, was a Pearl adorning the being of God before it was incarnated into the form of the Earth as we know it.

I don't know what this means, but I saw an image of a great Pearl opening up and all the myriad forms and wonders of the Earth spilled out for me to see. The Earth was this great Pearl inverted so that everything not visible on the inside became visible on the outside. He said that the intrinsic, essential energy form of the Earth is Pearl energy.

The Pearl is delicate like an egg. In the image you see, the Pearl is perfect and luminescent, and, at the same time, it is being held up by a force, the Serpent, that is swift, powerful, very watchful, and is also enormous compared to the Pearl. The Serpent could crush it in a moment with its jaws but it chooses to hold it up. The power of the Divine holds the Earth and all its kingdoms firmly in its grasp.

I see the Serpent now swaying with this Pearl in its mouth.

This swaying of the Serpent created the original trance that prepared the human race to carry out its purpose. In your chanting, you have often felt the swaying of the Serpent in an upward motion. This is the Serpent power that Undoes the trance of ego, of separation, that wakes you up from the Sleep of Forgetting

Can you see, the Earth itself is on a Path of incarnation, evolution and Return just as you are. In fact, your evolutionary process is not separate from Earth's evolutionary process. The Earth and everything on it is one organism. You are like one cell in the body of the Earth, but human beings have a hard time seeing themselves this way. The Earth in its entirety is a body. It has a Soul and an evolutionary path, just as you do, and as We said, they are not separate in Reality. The Earth will return to pure Pearl (Soul) energy one way or another, with or without man's conscious cooperation, consent and participation. Muktananda told you to direct your energy to the center of your forehead, to your Third Eye. It is in the Third Eye that the Wisdom of your shared evolutionary path is held and this is where it will be revealed to you.

The idea that the Earth has a Soul will be explained further as the writing unfolds.

The Serpent is a representative of the power of God. The Earth body as you know it is a very small and very beautiful organism that will, one way or another, at some time come to the end of its

evolutionary path, as We said. But no matter how that occurs,
nothing will be lost. What you have is the present opportunity.
The Earth will find its way into being in some form again, some form
you may not be able to imagine at the moment. Just as you will
find your way into another form when this body is gone, also a form
you may not now be able to imagine. What matters is that you
have the opportunity in this lifetime to participate in Earth evolution
in a way never before available to mankind. While you humans
might do great harm to the body of the Earth, you cannot hurt the
Soul of the Earth, and We are here to tell you that it is a great honor
and a great privilege to participate in Earth evolution rather than
Earth destruction. This is why We are speaking to you. We are
opening up a path of participation.

There is no way to describe the sense I am getting that in
the big picture, it doesn't matter at all what we do, and it
really matters tremendously, for us.

Today, with all we know about global warming alone, the
threats to the physical body of the Earth seem even greater
than when these words were written back in 1995. And I
experience that same paradoxical reality inside myself—it
really matters what I do with the opportunity and privilege
I have living on this beautiful planet, and, in the bigger scheme
of things, the Earth Soul and the Soul of Phyllis are immortal
and are not even separate, and together we move along our
evolutionary path whether I, Phyllis, decide to participate
in that evolution or not. And therefore, I go Home anyway,
with or without Phyllis's cooperation or consent. Mind-
boggling to the ego mind! Comforting on the one hand and
provocative on the other! Comforting that my welfare and
our ultimate collective welfare cannot be destroyed by this
human race. Comforting that I am a part of an evolution
of consciousness that is vast and cosmic and profoundly
loving and wise, whether I know it in any given moment or
not. Provocative because I hear the heartbeat of Mother

Earth crying for us to wake up from our Sleep of Forgetting, and I know I am not alone in that. Provocative because in my Phyllis personality, Soul's immortality is not an immediate enough answer to the pain I feel in the face of such great human suffering. I *want* to participate. And I believe that is exactly Their message — that both are true: what we choose really doesn't matter and, at the very same time, it *matters tremendously!*

We have said that the physical evolution of a life form on Earth occurs when that life form meets an obstacle to its continued survival and it must alter something within its own structure and functioning to survive overwhelming changing external conditions. This is the principle of physical evolution on Earth. Life forms that cannot make the needed changes and adaptations die out.

Like many other life forms, the human body has evolved and adapted itself to survive an enormous variety of changing and often life-threatening conditions. Many of the threats to your existence in the past arose from naturally occurring climate changes. Now suddenly you are faced with life-threatening climate changes that you yourselves have created.

*The impact you have on your external physical environment, **and** the extent to which you do not want to acknowledge the severity of it, **are the result of a changing internal psychological climate, the heating up, so to speak, of the power of ego consciousness**. As ego creates extremes of Domination and Submission, and as you continue to try to dominate the Earth itself without regard to the consequences, you yourselves are creating the conditions that now threaten your survival. It is in the face of these climate changes that you must **evolve now** if you want the human race to survive. Global warming is the outer manifestation of this inner heating up of ego consciousness.*

*This is the point: unlike all other living things on Earth, human beings took form to evolve **consciousness,** to evolve from a state of separation to a state of union, from ego consciousness to Soul* *consciousness. The end-game is not to evolve form: you did not come here ultimately to evolve body structure or technologies or philosophies, art or science, although all those areas of functioning are very necessary and important aspects of human evolution. You came ultimately to evolve* **consciousness.** *And the evolution of consciousness is symbolized by the Sand and the Pearl. This heating up of ego consciousness itself is now your most abrasive Sand.*

On the physical plane, when sand gets inside the oyster's shell and begins to cause irritation, the oyster coats that sand with a very smooth and luminescent substance. And it keeps coating it, layer by layer, until a pearl is created. **For humans, Sand is generated by the relentless difficulties, overwhelming obstacles, opposing forces and threats to your EGO existence that — necessitate adaptation and change to alleviate distress and ensure survival.** *Some examples of this Sand: struggles for food supply, safety and shelter, struggles with opposing opinions and beliefs, with experiences of rejection and betrayal, loss and grief.*

For ages and ages, human beings have, for the most part, attempted to coat these irritations or stressors with more and more elaborate adaptations of ego consciousness itself — technologies, social orders, religions, philosophies, etc. — which are certainly not always experienced as negative.

Often these adaptations are experienced as very constructive and effective means to certain ends. All these ways you attempt to coat the irritations of your ego consciousness are lawful. But because ego consciousness operates on the basis of Duality, whatever it devises, no matter how "good" it appears at any given time to any given group, there will never be lasting agreement about what is good, right or most effective. One person's good is another person's evil. History shows you again and again that what was deemed good yesterday can easily become anathema tomorrow. Therefore, more opposition, more friction, and therefore, **more Sand.**

When We speak of the Pearl you humans came here to create, We are talking about the flowering of Soul consciousness that comes from getting out of the play of Duality altogether by embracing and transforming all the resistance and friction that is found on the Horizontal Plane. This is the evolution of consciousness you came to participate in. This is what the Path of Supreme Surrender teaches you to do. The Earth will Return to pure Pearl energy with or without your participation, but you have been given this incredible opportunity to agree to participate.

Understanding that my greatest difficulties are actually the Sand around which my Soul came to make Pearls of Soul consciousness was a total reversal of everything I had believed up until then. I loved the image of the Sand and the Pearl, but it would be slow going to actually embrace the Sand that was mine. Embracing pain is not what ego wants to do. It wants to avoid, deny, resist, judge, blame, minimize, rationalize and project. My ego nature wanted to do all those things. The anxiety under my skin felt red-hot. I was still in the Fire.

What does it mean now to embrace the Sand that is OURS? Was the anxiety eating me up personally back in 1995 more than personal? Was it in fact one small part of the massive anxiety pushing on our collective awareness today? If embracing pain and fear were so very difficult for me in the face of my own individual trials, if it was so difficult for me to learn to stand in that Fire and not be burned but transformed, what will it take for us collectively to stand in the Fires we face together? Can we do it?

Hold the Guru inside you like the Serpent is holding the Pearl in his mouth, and walk with it. Walk with that absolutely delicate balance inside you between all the pressure and force and demands of daily life and the beauty of the essence of this Pearl inside you.

Listen to the Guru inside you and outside you and take all your energy and lay it at the Guru's feet and ask that it be used for your highest good and for the highest good and speediest Return of all.

...Last night I went to Satsang and because the chants have been so powerful for me lately, I wanted to have a similar experience again. But I let go of that and allowed myself to just feel empty. I'm practicing being with What Is in the small moments I remember. That seems to be the first step in embracing Sand. And then suddenly I again had a vision of the Serpent. His head shot out through my forehead and he was breathing out an enormous amount of Fire, turning his head in all directions. Then I saw him inside me, breathing Fire everywhere, as if burning up my "stuff," my baggage.

Muktananda told me that the stage I am in now does not last forever, that the process of burning my attachment to what I think is good and bad and my illusions of who I think I am, prepares the way for an emptiness I have never experienced. He said that as this empty space is created, the way energy will pass through me and the types of energy that will pass through me and the whole experience of it will change dramatically.

Later, I found out that the chant we were singing, called Kali Durge, was about two female goddesses, one of whom is Kali, who is fierce and burns up all your "stuff."

I chanted for a long time this afternoon. The little girl in me, the one who carries all this anxiety, was with me in the chant, and I was accepting that she is a part of What Is. So yes, I see that in learning how to be with What Is, I have to learn how to be with her. I have to find a way to embrace this anxiety and not run from it. I keep hearing, "God dwells within you as you" over and over and I try to see myself in all aspects, including "her," as a manifestation of God. Letting Muktananda take me out of despair and fear. He told me again to just breathe with him and it would all come and go exactly as it should. He said not to struggle so hard to figure it all out, that I will be given all the understanding necessary, as I have been given so far. It reminded me of something You said a long time ago. You said the river of your life flows on, with or without your consent; your choice is to *choose* what has already been chosen.

I was beginning to get it that Surrender to What Is requires fully accepting everything just as it is, without judgment. Being with what I experienced as Darkness was the first step in consciously choosing to clear out the places where I was blocked from the Light of Soul. This was what They meant by Surrender. This was the doorway to being of Service in the world. When Muktananda said to breathe in the sound of the chant, he was telling me to invite God into my house now, just as it is—and that would have the effect of clearing a Darkness I did not know was there. This was like shifting the Earth's axis as far as I was concerned.

Then again, I heard the voice of Muktananda, and he said, *What do you think enlightenment is — an old man sitting in a room meditating and having a few experiences?*

Clearly any thoughts I once had that spiritual development is characterized by instantaneous personal relief from all human suffering were replaced with a panorama of "participation" once inconceivable to me. I suddenly understood that the most wonderful moments of union with the Divine, on any level, are not ends in themselves. They are entry points into a world of Soul activation and participation beyond anything, in my consuming preoccupation with myself, I had ever heard or known. The magnitude of the task we have undertaken as human beings was impressed deeply into my awareness. and it wasn't about *me* anymore at all. At the very same time, it was all about me learning how to work with Sand. It was all about an entirely new definition of Surrender.

Chapter 5

The Truth Cannot Hurt You

S upreme Surrender is Surrender to What Is. And so I thought again of my parents. I had stopped communicating with them when the memories from my childhood became too jarring a contrast to the brief pleasantries of our Sunday morning phone calls. What would it mean to "breathe in" my experience of my parents? How could I hold to my truth *and* breathe through my fear of hurting them? I had no idea. I was so afraid of doing them harm. Though I was beginning to understand that we are all Souls and that we play the parts for each other that we agreed to play and that we are all Teacher for each other on the Road of Return, it was extremely difficult to hold onto that understanding in my day-to-day reality.

> I am aware of how much I still fear hurting my parents, especially my father, with my truth, how I still fear being seen as the crazy one, not being believed, of being accused of victimizing them.

*What you fear in your father is his pain. But you also know now that pain cannot kill you. See this pain as the Fire of Soul burning away all obstacles to Light and Love and Return. Just as fire on the physical level burns away matter and releases pure energy, **the Fire of the Soul burns away psychic or ego matter and releases Divine energy**. There is a process of transformation by Fire, in some form, at some time, for all matter as you know it. Fire is a symbol for truth. When you think of all the pain in your own* *life, much of it was your truth trying to reach you and inform you and guide you, doing battle with your resistance to it.*

Your resistance is based on misguided beliefs about the meaning of the experience you are having. In simple words, if the truth at a given moment is that you have a fatal disease, and you believe that means you must have deserved it, that you are burdening other people or that you will be missing experiences you were supposed to have, then you will resist this knowledge and burn in the battle between the right and wrong of it, the good and bad, the have and have not, or the fairness and unfairness of the situation.

You burn in resistance until all the untrue beliefs are burned away and you reach acceptance and true understanding. Which, in such a case, would be that when a person dies, their time on Earth has lawfully come to a close. They have had all the experiences on the Earth plane in that lifetime that they were supposed to have, and the particular death process they go through is one of those experiences. The truth in Our view is that no one is injured, but that those who grieve have come to have that human experience of loss and they have their own Fires to walk through on their own roads. This is true whether they understand it, accept it, believe it, or not.

*You still burn in relation to your parents because you believe your truth will hurt them. We say, from the perspective just given to you, that in Reality, **and you must be in Reality to see this**, you hurt no one. We told you about the Law of the Three In The One, which is one of the laws governing your existence. Just as there is a law called the Two in the One, there is also a law called the Three in the One. The Two in the One is manifested in your world as the Law of Duality – energies are divided into two opposite aspects of experience in ego consciousness that are then reunited in Soul consciousness. A known symbol for this is the Yin Yang. Just so, there is also a law called the Three in the One. This law manifests in more than one way for humans. The way We have already told you about is the Holy Trinity, which is a lawful interconnection between God, you (the Son), and the Holy Ghost. The Holy Ghost* *is all the rest of creation with which you interact on your journey through incarnation. It is like the totality of the Play you find yourself in with its set and scene, props, characters, story lines and themes. Your family in particular is the Holy Ghost that you are dealing with most profoundly right now, as it is for so many people. They are some of the central players in your particular human drama just as you are a central player in theirs. They are a part of what We call your Soul Circle. They are the Souls traveling most closely with you through lifetimes, each providing the others with the experiences asked for and needed on the journey through ego consciousness and on the Path of Return. They provide the arena in which, together, you create dense ego energies for your Karmic journey AND in which you also burn all ego energy up as you begin your ascent from the Horizontal Plane. See them as Teacher for you.*

You cannot avoid them. They came into body as much to experience you in your evolutionary Path as you came to experience them manifesting exactly as they are. We say again, you believe you will hurt your parents and We say that as a true fact that is not so. The truth cannot hurt anyone. It may anger or sadden or frighten their personalities, but it can do no real harm. You only hurt **yourself** *with your fear and your silence. You hurt everything in you that works so hard to live your truth. No one is spared anything worth sparing when another shields them from their truth. You know this.*

If God spared you from the truth of Divine Being, where would you be? *When God's Light illuminates the Darkness you have lived in, even if it hurts your eyes at first to see what that Light reveals, would you rather God spared you from the truth of* **your** *being? Would you rather remain in the Darkness of your deep belief that you had been left by the wayside on the road to Heaven? We know you would not. The wayside of the Road Home is rejection of your own truth. The point for you is this: You have said it yourself many times. The truth is always your friend. The truth is everyone's friend. There is nothing in the truth that can hurt you if you allow it into your being with a pure heart, and with a spirit of acceptance of any Fires that may need to burn along the* *way and in its wake. When you accept the Fires that burn to clear the way for Soul, you rise from the ashes in pure white light. This is about burning Consciously. This is your Path. This is what you came here in this lifetime to do. You have burned unconsciously untold times. Do you truly want to die in that state again? We think NOT.*

You will meet many Fires along this way and you are asked to walk through them all consciously. You ask it of yourself. Walking through a Fire means you acknowledge that there is an issue for you. It's not right or wrong, good or bad. It just is. You look at where old patterns of personality want to take over. For instance, you look at your tendency to hide, to split off from your Self, to conceal the parts of yourself that you doubt or believe are threatening, and then you try to become what you imagine others would approve of. You have done this many times before. This is not walking through the Fire; it is unconsciousness.

Walking through Fire means you listen to the call of your Soul above the roar of ego's resistance, hesitation, and fear, and you answer that call. Your particular Soul wants you to speak your truth to your parents and your personality, of course, does not. **Fire is the burning sensation you will feel when you do it, and Firepower is what will be released in the doing.**

Walking through Fire means you don't go anywhere, you stay right where you are and you do not retreat, you do not let yourself feel like an alien, you do not change the subject inside yourself. Walking through the Fire means not splitting off from Self, no matter what. It means staying with your truth and with the truth of Us no matter what — no matter what the effect on your behavior, and there will be an effect on your behavior in the world. When you are in ego, personality determines behavior. When you are in Self, Soul determines behavior. This will be extremely difficult at times for Phyllis Leavitt. She has confused living in Self and speaking from Soul with presumptuousness, danger and death. Walking through Fire means closing all the escape hatches and living in Self, speaking from Soul, anyway.

And so difficult as it was, and it *was* difficult, I began to see the concrete application of what They were talking about. There was no way I could continue to relate to my parents from the old me, the one who agreed to doubt herself, silence herself, and split off from her true Self. There was no way I could NOT listen to my Soul. I had not spoken to my parents for several months. It was time to face them. I told them they could come to Santa Fe and meet with T and me. The point was not to cut off contact forever — it was *to speak,* to tell them my truth, however much I could get out in their presence. This was the Fire I was learning to walk into — embracing my truth *and* embracing the response, whatever that might be. As for any Firepower that would be released, well, that remained to be seen.

I feel very disconnected from You lately. Maybe it's because my parents are coming.

How do you imagine God enters form? How do you imagine Divine Being tolerates the disconnection of incarnation? With Supreme Love — Supreme Acceptance, Supreme Understanding, Supreme Patience and Supreme Compassion. These are the very qualities that you are learning to develop in yourself. Without these qualities, you cannot tolerate the Fires of the manifest Guru. Without these qualities firmly and immovably in place, you will die as you have died before, and it is not your Soul's intent in this lifetime for this to happen. When We say die as you have died before, We mean that you will die in a state of self-doubt and of relinquishing your light to others. Every step you take out your door into the world of others and the challenges they represent on all levels, will call up the specter of disconnection as both the main threat and your main survival skill.

You lose yourself to others, to the fear of their judgment and to your own self-judgment. We do not say this as a criticism. We say it with Love because We know and you know, you came this time around to die quite differently.

Thank you. My parents are arriving this afternoon. Can you help me prepare for that?

*This is what We would like to share with you about their coming. Contrary to what you might think, the most important thing is not anything you might say or do. **The most important thing is where you live inside yourself in their presence.** Watch your eyes now. Make a distinction between giving your light away — allowing it to be taken by others — and shining light from your eyes as a conscious intent. This distinction will help you enormously. You will be able to keep your eyes open and at the same time, the inner door to your Soul will be closed to all energies you do not wish to take in and the door will also be closed to ego energies you do not want to project.*

*You can actually shine light into your parents' (or anyone's) Soul space. You can look beyond the form and shine light on the Path you have walked together and you can breathe with that. We are not saying that you can or should ignore the form. We are saying, **Go beyond the form. How do you think Christ forgave those who persecuted him? He was able to see through and beyond all form. If he had not been able to maintain that stance under the most extreme duress, he would not, essentially, have been the Christ. You understand? This is your road. If Christ had internalized the condemnation of his persecutors and hated them or himself, hanging on the Cross, he would not have been the Christ.***

I'm really trying to have that kind of Faith. I guess it's been long enough that I haven't spoken to my parents. I'm sure everyone is angry with me, but really, not speaking to them is not the point. It's about *talking*. It's so hard for me with my father. I sense his pain, and although he has never once expressed it in words, I want to spare him.

***

The first session went pretty well. They listened. I told them what sexual abuse had done to my life. My father cried. I didn't accuse them. I just said what I remembered without a lot of detail, about something that happened when I was a baby in a bassinet and about a basement memory. I just couldn't get myself to say anything more specific. All my mother said was that maybe it was the nurse they had for me when I was born, and the basement—well, if it happened, they didn't know anything about it.

I wouldn't say I was successful and not a total failure either. I managed not to give my energy away most of the time, or at least more than I would have been able to do without what You told me. At the same time, I took one look at my father's face and saw that very same look of great hurt and fear and I knew I could not say more. I felt exactly as I had before, instantly and deeply, that it would kill him, literally perhaps. I even questioned myself about exactly what it is I see in his face and why I see it there, and have for as long as I can remember, though it is barely conscious. And do I really see it or do I project it? I don't know.

They look older than the last time I saw them. I don't think they have any capacity to deal with my reality. They probably don't remember anything or won't or can't. On the other hand, somehow that perception reinforces my split self. How can it be, I hear myself asking inside, that they really were fine and yet I have carried so much pain all my life? At the same time, I still deny myself rather than them. I still give more weight to their apparent reality than to my own, and yet it is also better than before because I am watching myself and I am not just wide open. Can You help me?

*The fact that your struggle has come more fully into the light of consciousness is progress. Try, without saying or doing anything differently, to simply hold onto your truth more completely, with deliberateness. You see — **you do not have to confront them. You only have to confront the split in yourself, the place where you give your reality away, bury your truth, for the so-called sake of others.** THAT is what this is all about. Tell yourself you believe **yourself** and you will not forsake **yourself**, that you will not leave yourself by the wayside of your own Soul's Path. You see it is not about you forsaking God. It is not about denying anything external. It is about **not denying yourself**, in that holy intersection where you and Soul and Us and Christ and God are one. When you can do this, the road will go more smoothly.*

Feel your own light inside you. Practice it with your parents. You needn't say anything out loud to them, now or ever, as far as We are concerned. Your own Soul will make that decision and there is no wrong decision. If your parents died tomorrow and you never got the opportunity to say anything to them in the flesh in this life, rest assured that the opportunity to love Self and believe Self, speak from Self and not abandon Self will not be diminished in any way. It will be given to you, in this life, in ample measure.

The energies you and your parents are working out are not limited to the temporary bodies you now inhabit. Do you honestly believe that this communication can take place only in the flesh? Do you not think it can occur across boundary lines of incarnation, with one in body and the other out of body, or both out of body? Of course it can. Look at your intersection with Us! Clearly, We are not in body and you are! Must you continue to believe that you can protect them or anyone from his or her destined, chosen path? Try as an experiment, if you can, to speak your truth clearly inside you mind in their presence. Just try it.

I tried what You suggested about stating my truth inside me, not forsaking myself. It wasn't really that hard to do. What I experienced was this. I felt whole at moments around them in a way I haven't before. I felt separate and whole and alive and I didn't feel like the hurt alien one. I didn't feel split and at war with myself as I have in the past. I no longer felt like I had a dark secret and I didn't feel like I had to choose between their truth and mine. I chose mine, and I felt free, like it really didn't matter to me at all anymore if they understand me or not, if they ever enter my world at all.

But I am wondering if I am in denial. I fear I have just sold out in some subtler and more disguised way. Am I a coward? But the truth is, I felt good. I feel good. I have my world and my reality, which is growing and deepening every day and there are no words to say thank you that I have You. I understand that what I did with them today is exactly what I need to do in the world, with everyone and everything I meet—which is not forsake myself, not condemn myself, but hold onto my truth. I see that it is essentially an internal process. I don't know that I have ever come this close to not feeling split before. I'd like to believe wholeheartedly what You said about the communication not necessarily having to be done in the flesh.

This is the solidity that can come only from the acceptance of the whole of one's truth of Being. This is forged from hard work, perseverance, faith, hope and grace. It is not just an attitude or a thought process or a desire. This is one example of Pearl formation on Earth. This is what you are doing.

You asked, How can I hold them in love and keep my truth at the same time? *And so you see that you simply continue to be with What Is. Walk through this Fire and drop all preconceptions of what it is supposed to look like. You think you are supposed to be tortured through all this. Do you believe that Christ's experience was torture on the Cross? Christ held back nothing in speaking his truth to the world, addressing the hypocrisy, greed, untruths and inhumanity of his times, fiercely, and without fear of consequences to himself. Yet when Judas betrayed him, he raised not a finger, spoke not a word to prevent it. What was, was meant to be. This he knew and had accepted long before the final hours approached.* **There is no inconsistency in accepting your parents' role in your life unless you believe there is. There is nothing else but to accept their role in your life.** *The torture you impose is self-doubt. Peace, even in extreme circumstances, lies in listening to the voice of Soul and following where it leads you. All will unfold. Be patient with yourself, trust in your own Soul for guidance, have faith, and continue to walk this road with Us. Lifetimes are converging. Let them converge. Let them do their work of Undoing with you and for you. Nothing can hurt you, not even death.*

The second session with my parents and T didn't go so well. My mother had time to sleep on it and she came into the session as the angry victim of an accusing daughter, after all they had done for me...T did not take an active role. But after we got back to my house, my parents and I talked and I did tell my mother more about the least threatening of all my memories. She said she didn't remember any of it, and of course my father didn't either. But at the end of the conversation, she hugged me and said that if she had done what I described, she was sorry.

Perhaps it was lame on my part that I didn't have the courage to say more. I have such a hard time with the pain I see in my father's face. But the small apology I got from my mother really felt like all I needed. For whatever reason, I suddenly don't feel I have to say more. I broke the spell of silence. Whether they acknowledge anything ever is no longer the point. I broke the spell of silence for myself. They saw the raw pain I have kept hidden from them all my life and they heard me say where I believe it came from. And that seems to be enough. I highly doubt I will ever tell them any more.

At the very same time, I fear I failed the test and I feel like the sorriest Soul in the universe. My mother really seems to feel that *I* had the problem and that it was *me who hurt her*, criticized her and rejected her. But our conversation didn't escalate into hostility and she didn't flip over into anger. I stayed with myself and I was as honest as I was able to be and I didn't take any responsibility for anything that I didn't feel was mine. I also didn't try to make them like me.

Yes, I didn't say anything to my father and he didn't ask, and after they left there was a moment when I felt like I could get very critical of myself for that. But I didn't. I was able to step back and say I did a big thing, and even though it was not complete, what I did was great progress.

The way I see it, the progress wasn't even so much that we had the conversation. It was that I did not abandon myself, I didn't doubt my truth, and I held my ground and let my mother have the feelings she had. I didn't feel I had to fix it but I also didn't feel cold or uncaring. I felt compassionate and it was okay, because I loved myself through it all. I believe there is Soul operating through all this. My faith and my trust feel like they have skyrocketed. You are here to guide me. You guided me through all this with my parents in the most profoundly wise way. I am beginning to have more trust that You are here and won't leave me.

I heard You tell me last night to remember that my parents have incarnated several times themselves since the witch lifetime and that I can keep in mind that they are not exactly the same people they were in that life, that the pattern pervades but that they are moving along their own line of Karma and evolution at their own rate.

There are no accidents. Every Soul in body has the very same perfection of inner and outer circumstances. Trust this. This is the truth.

I do hear You, but how can my weakness and fear with my parents be perfect?

*It is not weakness. **The object of Sand is not judgment; it is Pearl formation.** This occurs layer by layer over time. It is not an instantaneous process. You are given the Sand you need for the evolution of your own Soul's consciousness. The fact that you feel pain at not being ready to say more is exactly the work of Sand. If you felt no discomfort, nothing would change, no movement would happen. Bow to this. Do not attempt to avoid it in any way. Do not, as in so many past lives, succumb to self-hatred. Feel the resistance over and over for as long as Soul tells you to feel it. Act when Soul tells you to act. Bow to what you call suffering and stay in that bowed position as long as Soul tells you it is necessary for whatever Work of Undoing you are engaged in.*

When you fully dare to feel your own pain and anguish over this issue, you will be able to deal with their pain and anguish, not because your personality will ever particularly want to, but because Soul will guide you and Soul will Redeem that pain in you, and ironically, it will no longer feel like pain. Do you understand? Soul will not force you to deal with it. That would be impossible. That would be to say that Soul would operate with the energies of Domination and Submission, and this is not possible. Soul, God, your Guides, do not force anything.

The Angel of Destruction is standing over your shoulder at this very moment, pushing down the walls of the false temple in which you were forced to pray, forced to acquiesce, and forced to die. Let it fall. Help her do her work. She asks for your participation, she calls you from her fiery position. There is nothing to fear. Only light can issue forth from this apparent Darkness.

***

The glimmer of a Pearl in the Darkness. Perhaps the experience with my parents was giving me a sense of what Pearl formation could mean. Guided by my Soul and by You, I did my best to take the extreme distress of my relationship with my parents, that Sand, and I "coated" it with the luminescence of holding onto my truth. A tiny step, perhaps, but the Pearl that began to form was the experience of wholeness, of the splits inside me healing. The Pearl that began to form was the beginning of a foundation for my Soul to live and breathe in the body, the vehicle, that is Phyllis.

Chapter 6

Bow to Everything

Several months had passed since the writing began. I had been working as a psychotherapist in private practice for six years, divorced for eight, and only my youngest son, Daniel, lived at home. The agonizing anxiety and panic, bouts of inexplicable nausea, and fears of leaving my house that bordered on agoraphobia, continued. Going to the grocery store was sometimes as far from home as I could get, and even there I often had to breathe my way through the aisles — breathing out darkness and breathing in love over and over again — just to make it through the checkout counter and home.

I would consciously leave my hurting child self in a walled off place inside me while I worked with clients, and I would promise her I would come for her when my day was done, if only she would leave me alone in the meantime. In reality, all that really meant was that I asked her not to overwhelm me with anxiety during the day, to let me work and "appear normal." Looking back, I don't know how I managed to do that, but somehow I did.

There must have been an agreement, whether I was aware of it or not, that I would go where They took me. I believe I made that agreement before I was born as Phyllis. I had opened the door to Them, to a truth of Divine Love and Being that was undeniable, and as a result, I opened the door to all the other truths that came with it, that were in fact inseparable from it and took me straight into the Fires that were mine. There was nowhere else to go.

And so, having asked entrance, and having been instructed to breathe with all that is, however haltingly I was able to do it, I was taken further and further into the Fire.

I had a terrible day filled with body memories that were so intense I felt physically nauseous. You said You loved me and You said:

*Hold sacred absolutely every aspect of your being, even the horrible feelings and the confusion and the desire to repress. **Bow down to EVERYTHING. There is NOTHING ELSE. The essence of true spiritual work is THIS and nothing else. All doors to heaven open through this route.***

I feel like I am getting it, like the stark yet absolutely cosmic simplicity of it is sinking in. There is nowhere to go but through. At best, I take a few breaths.

I got up this morning and went outside to write and this is what You told me.

*When you hold sacred every aspect of your being, there can be no separation from Us or from anything. You see, one of the main separations you are working on is the separation from the pain, the memories, the body, the wish to leave the body. **When We told you that you cannot breathe yourself into the mind of God unless you walk through all your fears and doubts, We meant exactly that. This is a PROFOUND teaching that you are being given. God lives within you just exactly as you are.***

When you breathe with Us, whether you breathe with the Plant World or Muktananda or you breathe God into yourself, you intensify your process along your Path. This is a law of how the universe operates. God breathed the world into existence just as God will also breathe it out of existence. Breath that is aligned with God acts on the breather as an agent of intense movement in the psyche and in the spirit. You need to know that the breathing you have done so far has radically expanded your awareness, and is responsible for all the major earthquakes in your psyche. You need to know that the work you do in one area — for instance, breathing with the Plant world — that work, if done with a pure heart and no ulterior motives, will connect you to every other aspect of your work in a Real way. In other words, when you enter Our world, and you follow Our messages, you will connect, at the proper time for you, to all other avenues of truth necessary to your Path. For instance, you will, of necessity connect to past lives, to Soul patterns, to further spiritual instruction and Teachers, to Earth kingdoms and the Elements, etc., as you have seen. It is not accidental that so many doors have opened. It is how this works. Nothing is accidental. The farther you go, the more you will become conscious of the connections.

Perhaps all the breathing I was doing in this new way was literally fanning the flames of the Fires that awaited me.

*So you hear Us say that it is time for you to walk through many Fires. This is the time when you must translate this Divine teaching into practice. We are not speaking only about meditation and chanting or writing or doing readings, although these practices are of course invaluable. We are talking about **walking through YOUR Fires**. You must meet this crying child inside you because you are still separate from her and you fear her, and the unconscious desire to continue to split her off is the most powerful inner Fire you now face, more powerful than the fears of what other people may think or the fear of craziness.*

The crying child inside you is the psychic embodiment of the unconscious aspects of all your past lives, all previous incarnations. *We described Phyllis Leavitt as made up of shreds of past forms. That description includes the voices of derision* *and destruction that you have absorbed.* **What you call the inner child is the core essence of all the Soul Parts, all the unresolved aspects of past lives, that you carry with you into this life.** *We gave you the image, the symbol, of putting all those Soul Parts in a circle around you and consciously lighting the Fire under them yourself, dying those deaths* **consciously** *now. We said they are all, in one form or another, trapped in their ashes and you are to light the Fire that will set these Soul Parts free. This is a Healing Image, a road map through the Wilderness of the Horizontal Plane. What We give you is a guide along the road you are now traveling, but it is not the journey. It is a precious Map. Only you can walk the road.*

The crying child inside me was indeed a core essence of experience much greater than the child Phyllis. It was she whose body shook uncontrollably as memories surfaced, both from this life and other lives. It was she who feared heresy and wanted me to be silent. At the very same time, she was wrapped around my Soul, and answering her cries meant opening the door once again—and opening it wider—to exactly that which had gotten me killed in the witch life. To answer her cries, I had to let God and Soul speak. It was an exquisite dilemma. Soul asked me to stand in Fire this time and not be burned. Die consciously now, They told me. And dying consciously and walking through Fire were synonymous. We were talking about big Fire.

Lie down on the Earth and receive healing energy to the hurting body. The Earth wishes to help. The Earth wishes to share her love with you and everyone, to be present with you and travel this road with you just exactly as you have wished and extended yourself to travel with her. What We give you is not a spiritual doctoral thesis or a psychic technology. It is Soul Work. Do you see?

You are working at bringing Light into a very Dark place in yourself. That is one of your Fires. Fire takes different forms for different people, but whatever the form, **there is nowhere to go but** *into it. And as We have shown you, there is nowhere to go but OUT THE OTHER SIDE. Let the Darkness into you. In fact, it already has entrance, but you make it conscious and willing now by accepting that it is already there, and then you let it pass out of you. As you do this, you both transform the Dark energy into Light and you give back, energetically, the ego energy of Darkness to those from whom it came so that they may do the same thing with it that you are doing. If you fear it, if you reject it, it stays with you. If you believe We can give you armor strong enough to keep it out, then this is a misunderstanding.*

We keep nothing Dark out, nor do We absorb any of it. This is the essence of Redemption. Horizontal Plane energy is Redeemed.

Their definition of Redemption is reclaiming and transforming *energy* for Soul and the Creator, not saving people from sin. They have no concept of sin at all; there are only levels of consciousness — ego consciousness and Soul consciousness. Darkness belongs only to ego. Redemption is the process by which ego consciousness is transformed into Soul consciousness, or the process by which ego releases its hold on the psyche so that Soul can fill the vehicle and radiate its Divine Love.

I have to say here that once again it was very frightening to have these ideas conveyed in Biblical language. I could only imagine the consequences if I had ever talked like this in my witch life. And although I had never been a part of any church in this life, I still felt great fear at the thought of anyone knowing I was speaking this language.

Nevertheless, I could sense the implicit power of willingly passing Darkness through myself rather than resisting it. But it would take everything I had and a lot of help from Above to do what They were asking.

What does this mean specifically for you right now? It means bow down to this crying child inside you. Love her and honor her as you have never done before. Love her body, not just as a concept but as a physical act. Caress her, adorn her, talk to the body, sing to her, chant into her, for the purpose of making it totally safe, totally acceptable, for her to release her pain and let it pass through you. These are very difficult instructions. Who in their right mind wants to stand in such a Fire and believe they will not be burned, will not die in these flames but be reborn? When you are living in the Shadow of the Holy Ghost, this Fire of Redemption is not understood and you human beings seem to be in a desperate struggle to shove your neighbors into the Fire in an illusory effort to save yourselves or "save" them. And you really believe it will work!

*Accept the pain of your wounds totally. Know that pain for what it is. It is not a cause for shame or blame. It is not a defect or a curse. It is the Shadow of the Holy Ghost, **which everyone must confront**, must look in the eye and not turn away from, not circumvent or minimize in any way. You know the image of a knight taking out his sword and slaying a Fire-breathing dragon. We give you a different image. Breathe the dragon's Fire in, totally, and pass it through, totally. It will pass through you and it will be transformed by your total acceptance and by your total lack of fear. **Fear and resistance and denial are the foods it eats.** Let it find no food in you and it will pass out.*

*Another image is that of a believer holding out a Cross for protection from evil, and the evil one is then burned or driven back by the power of the Cross. The image of one holding out a Cross in the face of Darkness is a real Healing Image, but the meaning has been lost over time. This is the true meaning: the Cross is a symbol of your transformation from a Horizontal Plane existence to a Vertical ascent to Oneness. When you hold the Cross in front of you, you are transforming the projected ego energies coming at you from others (which is the Shadow of the Holy Ghost). These ego energies are projected in an attempt to influence and control your mind or your body or your feelings. **When you pass energy through the Cross, you are extracting the pure energy of these*** *projections from others and also your own projections onto them and onto yourself. You are meeting Shadow energy with Soul energy. You engage with that Shadow energy with the force and the Light of Soul. You don't fight it or curse it or run from it. When you allow this dense Horizontal Plane or ego energy to pass through your Cross, it is transformed, blessed, and all that ego energy is made available for use by Soul. This is what Blessing truly is. This is how transformation truly occurs. Ego energy is transformed into Soul energy. Ego's will is released to God's Will. No one is pushed back or burned. The ego projections of others simply do not land as intended. And others will be left with their projections and they will do with that whatever they are able to do.*

You see, you humans have interpreted this mythic image of one holding out the Cross as Good conquering Evil. But there is no war with Evil in Our world, in Reality. Divine Love does not conquer, it does not kill and it knows no enemy. Divine Love illuminates, and in that illumination, it transforms. When you work with the Cross the way We describe, when you breathe Divine Love into your own system, through your own system, and out into the world, everything in its path is lit up with that Love.

I take very small breaths in this new way. I breathe in only as much as I can stand. I entertain the possibility of standing in a Fire that has felt like certain death to me, one small flame at a time. I can't imagine how anyone, even Jesus, carried an actual Cross, but there are small moments when I hold the vision of my Cross in front of me.

Chapter 7

The Clouds Speak

*I*t may very well be impossible to truly convey what life was like for me during this time. I literally lived in two different worlds. My daily life was very difficult. Although there were certainly moments of greater peace and even feelings of "normalcy" at times, for the most part, anxiety and panic lay in wait for me as soon as I wasn't totally occupied. A nameless, faceless sense of dread woke me in the night and clawed at my heart and throat. The feeling of foreboding was getting stronger, not abating. I don't think I even tried to explain it to myself. I was holding on for dear life. I went in and out of feeling "crazy." I could not make logical sense of my existence. But through it all, They were my lifeline. When They spoke to me, it was as if my heart and brain opened into an entirely different universe. I *saw* my life and all of life through the lens of Divine meaning, purpose and connection. I was allowed into Divine Heart and Mind, and the understandings that were given to me reverberated, literally vibrated, in a place of Truth inside me. At moments it was as if Phyllis was not there at all. I still knew I was Phyllis, but she was the shell inside which a Pearl was asking to be formed, and the luminescence of Pearl blasted a Love not of this world through my heart. At these most blessed moments of Grace, I found myself sobbing. They were not tears of sadness or even joy. They were the tears of a heart breaking open, and the desire to be a servant of this Grace was all there was… And then, back into the Fire once more.

In yet another moment of reprieve, the voice of Mother Earth opened my vision once again and brought cool water to the Fires I was already standing in and to the Fires I could not yet see.

> Evening. I went walking with my dog tonight and when I looked up at this huge dark cloud with silver sunlight around the edges, I felt I should write when I got home. I'm asking entrance, Cloud friends.

The Clouds say, *We are an organic extension of the veins of the Earth, the waters you stood in* (this refers to my experience of Baptism in a little stream in Tesuque, NM, described in Book I), *the oceans that nurtured the embryo of life as you know it. We are Water element. We are the water-heart of the Earth. We exist as a Circle just as you are a part of many Circles and the One Circle. We are water serving one of her many purposes, just as you are flesh serving many purposes. Just as water takes many forms, so you take many forms in the great rounds of your Circles. But you do not seem to know what your many forms are or what your many Circles are as we do. Like the plant world, we of the water world love our form and our function.*

We do nothing but breathe with God. We do not live in time as you know it, but we know time. We reflect the ever-changing light and atmosphere around us but we are always the same. You are thinking to yourself that pollution surely changes us but you are wrong. Man is sadly poisoning the Earth and will limit its use in the future for himself and all creatures, but we are never poisoned. We just reflect back to you what you have created (as so much of your world does), as surely as we reflect the light of the sun in a variety of colors.

Be like us. Reflect back to yourself and to others the purity of sunlight and moonlight. Breathe with God constantly. Know what Circles you are a part of and take joy in those Circles as well as in your own breath. Be like us on a sunny, breezy day and transmit the essence of peace. Be like us in the heart of a storm and transmit the Fire of God in the sky like we do. We are born from water vapor and we give birth to rain and snow and sleet and hail, and they give birth to rivers and oceans who then give birth to water vapor. **That is our Circle, and just like a circle, it doesn't, in Reality, begin or end anywhere.** *Think about that for yourself. You are a part of many Circles, and just like a circle, you don't begin or end anywhere.*

We ask you, at what precise moment does water vapor become a cloud? You would say when it is visible to the human eye. But we do not see it that way. There is **no** *moment in time when water vapor becomes us, the clouds. We exist* **as a complete Circle** *all the time. That is the only way we know how to put this into words. See with our eyes. The waters of the oceans and the rivers and the lakes, and the vapors that rise from them, and we the clouds, so to speak, and the rain and the hail and the snow — we are* **one being, one being in a multitude of forms at all times, at the same time**, *and we know ourselves as that. We may appear to be speaking to you as clouds over the tops of these trees, but we are in our entire Circle in consciousness always.*

We are Water element. And water is simultaneously sleet, rain, snow and vapor, puddle, ocean, river, lake and stream. We are Water first and individual manifestations of water secondarily, momentarily. In physical form, you are Soul first, Phyllis Leavitt or your witch self or any and all of your many incarnate forms and personalities only secondarily, momentarily.

We love life as God created it on Earth. We are honored to serve the functions our Circle serves. We are a primary element of the particular life forms of the Earth, like a primary color. And we take joy in that and we will continue to take joy in that until we all Return together.

You human beings are not a primary color. You are a complex configuration of many elements. The main difference between you and us is that you live in time, in your consciousness, that is.

We do not. In your body, certainly you live in time, but in your consciousness, well, that is something of a matter of choice. This is another aspect of what the human race in particular came to work with. Time, as it is counted and calculated and deified by human beings, has cultivated in you an extremely dangerous near-sightedness. The distortion of time is one part of the Sleep of Forgetting, one part of what keeps your eyes shut to the greater Circles of which you are a part, because you, too, are a part of many Circles.

We clouds are, as you know, a very thin veil between Earth and a greater view of the cosmos. Just as Earth sometimes needs a break from the intensity of the sun and needs the coolness of our shadow and the moisture we bring to everything that grows, just in that way you, too, sometimes need a break from the intensity of the sun. When we are in the way of your vision of the infinite sky, let that be a gentle reminder to you that it is a part of your functioning to move back and forth between the microcosm and the macrocosm and that our appearance signals focus on the microcosm. Bring your vision down to the surface of the Earth, down to the very particulars of yourself. Then let water, the purity of water, literally and symbolically wash over you.

Never be afraid that the sun will not reappear. Just as the sun seems to go behind a cloud, it only appears that way to you. It has not gone anywhere. It is where it always was. Snows melt and puddles evaporate but water is not gone. It is just gone from your particular view in that particular form at that particular time. Do you understand? **You are no different. When you "die," you are no more gone than the sun. Believe this. We are here to tell you there is no such thing as death. There is only trans-formation.** *That is one Great Circle we are all a part of. Discover the Circle of your own life, of your own incarnations. Discover where your Circle intersects with others and merges with everyone's.*

We, your friends from so many directions, are here to tell you from every angle we can find that we are not going anywhere. We have been here for "millions of years." Just as we say to you, is there any chance the sun will not come up tomorrow? So we say to you that we will be here. And when that particular tomorrow comes that your particular sun does not rise in your particular heavens, you will be gone away where the energy of that sun has gone. Do you understand what we are trying to tell you? It isn't a foreign language we speak, it is only that we speak it in a different sense of time.

And so the concept of Circles was expanded and opened like another great substructure of our human existence. I understood that we have a Circle of our own Incarnations and a Soul Circle, those we travel with through lifetimes, and that we are in a Circle with all our Teachers and all the elements and kingdoms of the Earth... But I had never before seen or felt what the clouds said that day — that we are like water, and in Reality we exist in all our many forms at once, that we are Soul first and individual identities only secondarily, momentarily. Through Them, I have been given a glimpse of that Reality — Phyllis Leavitt is only one small part of my Circle of Incarnations, I have Soul Circle connections with others through lifetimes, and I am in a Circle of self, guru and God. I have a sense of myself that is beyond this one life and that gives me comfort and a vastly expanded sense of the greater Reality in which I walk my personal path.

I'm amazed at how much I feel on so many levels. I feel physical sensations when the clouds are speaking, just as I do when You are speaking. I *feel* the thought forms and the images and the meanings. You are a miracle to me.

Man's understanding of the word "miracle" is only a representation of his limited understanding of the laws of the universe. The word miracle implies that something that could not possibly happen occurs anyway. This is not true. Many miraculous things happen when you move out of one set of apparent laws and into another set of un-apparent laws.

Chapter 8

The Law of Eating: White and Black Magic

My sister and her family went on a road trip through the Southwest, and my two sons and I met them in Colorado. We were camping in Ouray when an unexpected difficult encounter provided the opening for an absolute flood of light.

I would like to go back to something I began writing on the trip. Is that okay?

There is no time in this space. There is no right time and no wrong time. All of that, including your question, is irrelevant. When you breathe with Us more continually, you will not be plagued by these unnecessary rituals of approach to the Divine Being that you are.

Okay. On the trip, there was something big that happened. The man who owned the campground where we stayed got furious at Eddie because he had apparently accidentally driven over a curb. The man came to our campsite and went into a rage and wouldn't stop. There was no right thing to say to him. He took everything we said, including Eddie's sincere apology, and just hurled it back at us. He let us know in no uncertain terms that he could kick us out right then and there. But I think he got thrown off balance by the fact that not one of us engaged in a fight with him. We all apologized and asked repeatedly what we could do. It seemed like he wanted a fight so that he could exert his power as the owner. But when none of us gave him that fight, he finally looked deflated and walked away.

I didn't say a word, but I couldn't shake it off and within minutes I was completely beside myself. I was unable to talk to anyone, including my sister, who tried to ask me what was wrong. I just went into my tent by myself and cried. When I look back on it, it seems like it wasn't only the level of his anger that undid me. It was the ignorance in it and the blind need to destroy the target of his anger AND our powerlessness to be heard or really do anything at all. Like the offense was not that great but the sentence was still death.

I tried to breathe through the Cross inside myself and let his rage pass through me, but even so, I went right into an old trance and I could not pull myself out. Everyone else was able to handle it much better than I did. My sister later told me they sat around the fire and had a really good talk together. At least I understood why I was so devastated, so I wasn't too hard on myself. I knew that enormous fear of an angry authority was flooding in from the past.

Perhaps the veil between my lifetimes was incredibly thin, I don't know. That sounds so melodramatic and self-indulgent, but my emotional reaction to the campground owner was beyond anything even I would consider normal. I was completely out of present time. I was projecting a life and death fear onto him that had nothing at all to do with anything actually happening, but it was exploding in my body as if he was the judge and jury of the Inquisition, as if he were holding the torch to my stake. Perhaps the whole experience illustrates the validity of what They call our Circle of Incarnations — that we carry with us all the unresolved pieces of past life experience into our present lives as "memory," and these "memories" can either be the fuel for more of the same Karmic experience or they can help us understand what issues we need to work through now. For me, melodramatic or not, there was no doubt I had huge unresolved issues from my witch life.

Even saying all this today, I feel like the weirdest person. Why do you have to inflate a stupid reaction that could just mean you regressed to some toddler part of yourself that was afraid of mommy or daddy yelling? Why do you have to make it a past life memory or some big Soul issue? And all I can say is that is what I experienced — it felt as if there were a death sentence right inside the rage of the campground owner and I felt it in my body. Looking back, I am sad to this day that I was not able to be a normal part of my family sitting around the campfire having a meaningful conversation together about a crazy incident.

The next morning I woke up before everyone else and I went to the little outdoor café at the campground to write. The owner was quietly serving pancakes. When I went up to the counter to get coffee, he didn't seem to have any recollection that I was one of the people he had been screaming at the night before. Maybe it was completely over for him. It was not over for me.

So, I sat down to write.

> Why would anyone, even Christ, choose as a Soul, a path of persecution? If Supreme Surrender is Surrender to What Is, then that has to mean Surrender to **everything** that Is, including war, hate, persecution, murder — what so many people are experiencing and have been for so long. Why would a Soul choose to incarnate as a slave, a woman forced into sex trafficking, an orphaned child, a victim of the nuclear bomb at

Hiroshima? You said that Fire is the great purifier. What is this process of purification about? What is it that needs to be purified?

So, let Us start here. Yes, this is difficult for the human mind in its present state to comprehend. That is why you have not read or heard an explanation that satisfies you. It is really not an issue of receiving an adequate explanation, if you can accept that. Otherwise, the answer to that question would be well known and perhaps would influence human behavior for the better. But obviously that is not the case. For instance, the concept of original sin doesn't seem to help the human race change its behavior in terms of aggression and self-destruction.

You are asking why what you call "evil" exists in the world, why people behave as they do. You are asking what you and so many others are actually working through and Redeeming by traveling this Path of Persecution as We have called it and as you have experienced it to be. We do not use the word evil. We say there is no evil; there is only ignorance. We say there is no evil; there is only the Sleep of Forgetting the Source. And We say that ignorance and sleep in this sense have great power to determine actions and events on the Horizontal Plane.

It is a DIVINE INTENT that informs the path of incarnation, *whether of a single individual or an entire species or galaxy. What We can say right now is that the intent for humans was to travel a particular path of separation and reunion, like finding yourselves lost in a great unknown and having to find your way back.* **Ego consciousness is the condition of separation you took on to make this journey; this is the Sleep of Forgetting.** *As individuals, as a race, and as a planet, whether you know it or not, you are striving to align yourselves with and become consciously aware of the intent now to Return, to wake up from this Sleep of Forgetting AS NEVER BEFORE.*

The Laws of Gravity, the laws that create ego consciousness, are what created the original state of separation in human beings. We are here to help you understand ALL the Laws of Gravity in order to make this journey Home, to help you understand what created the Sleep of Forgetting in the first place and what you can do to wake up from it.

Mankind is an outgrowth of the animal kingdom, and while this fact is obvious, it is generally overlooked by human beings because you tend to think of yourselves as an entirely separate species. **You must know yourselves as animals.** *Does that sound strange to you? It is a very profound truth. Part of your Sleep of Forgetting the Source is forgetting which kingdom you belong to. How many times in your life have you really considered what it means to be animal in nature? Many religions preach that man must overcome or tame his animal nature. Not only do We not agree, We do not see that any of that preaching has changed behavior in any real or helpful way. You have chosen to ignore, judge, try to overcome, "rise above" or totally indulge your animal nature, or you excuse certain behaviors on the basis of your animal nature.*

You must know your place in the great scheme of things from many angles. The animal kingdom is one of the Circles you are in. You cannot continue to unconsciously imagine that you are separate from that kingdom, **but you must also understand your animal nature from a new point of view.**

You did not come here to Earth to become Superman or robotic or "pure spirit" free of body. **You did not come to Earth to leave the animal kingdom in any way.** *The animal kingdom agreed to operate on certain principles when it took form. One of those principles was that bodies would be born and bodies would die. One of the principles of incarnation altogether is that the Infinite Divine Creator takes* **finite** *form. This is the Law of Mortality.*

We tell you now about yet another powerful force of Gravity. We call it **The Law of Eating.** *It is critical for you to understand that* *the animal kingdom also agreed to operate on the principle of EATING, eating from the plant world and the mineral world and from the animal world of itself as well. This is an essential part of the condition of Mortality. If this agreement had not been made, these ways of sustaining life temporarily in form would not exist. You must eat to stay alive. It is not evil when a wolf kills and eats a rabbit or a lion eats a zebra. It is not evil when you eat a chicken or vegetables. In the animal kingdom and in the plant kingdom, this is an agreed upon form of cooperation. And the water world and the mineral world have made the same agreement to cooperate and participate in the feeding required for continued incarnation in finite form.*

*As animals, you are always eating. The most obvious form of · eating involves physical food. **But you humans are different from all other animals and all other life forms on Earth, because you alone have an ego consciousness. You alone have an ever evolving and increasingly strong sense of a separate self that REQUIRES not only physical food but also emotional, mental and what you call spiritual food. It is this agreement in regard to the Path of human beings that sets you apart from all other animals and has determined the forms you are now taking—the size of the brain, the structures of communication, the experimentation in social organization, tool development, the complexity of emotion, intellect and spiritual striving, etc. Not the other way around.** It is not a blind force of evolution that has created the human creature as you know it. It is a condition of incarnation into ego consciousness that you hunger for, and that you are compelled to seek out and devour each other's emotional, mental and what you call spiritual energy all the time, in addition to the physical food you need to keep your physical body alive.*

*The Law of Eating is one of the most powerful forces of Gravity there is. It conditions you to ceaselessly eat whatever can be gotten on **all** the above-mentioned levels of your existence, **and not necessarily ask permission to dine.** Sex, too, has become part of the food that is continuously sought, not only for the sake of animal* *procreation, but to serve all the other ways you attempt to get energy from one another – and as We said, with or without permission. If you can understand this, this way of eating is neither bad nor good. It is **lawful** for ego consciousness to function this way. The lion does not ask the zebra if it would like to become dinner. The lion was made to survive by eating zebras and all the other animals it can catch. Within the condition of Mortality, most of your world operates on the basis of "eat and/or be eaten." On that level, the grasses have agreed to be food for the zebra and the zebra has agreed to be food for the lion. And it is no different for you humans with the diverse food sources you require for your **ego** existence. Ego's relentless need to "capture" and eat all the energies other human beings contain is how ego consciousness was created to survive and thrive. At the very same time, the individual zebra would prefer not to become the lion's lunch; the individual human would prefer not to be prey for an economic, emotional, religious or sexual predator. But what We are trying to tell you is that in your Horizontal Plane existence, in ego consciousness, it is **inevitable** that you will have predator and prey. One will dominate and another will be subdued. This is the Duality of Domination and Submission. Ego's need to dominate in order to get its many needs and desires met will inevitably meet the resistance of those preyed upon. Individual prey will continue to flee the hungry predator, be eaten, fight back, or turn around and overcome their pursuers. And thus, the Duality of Domination and Submission continues.*

*From ego's point of view, it is not desirable to be the prey. And while predatory behavior is often judged as "bad" and punished, it is also **very often justified and rewarded**. This widespread phenomenon of eating without permission is a FACT of your existence in an animal body and in ego consciousness. This is what We mean when We say that this way of eating is neither bad nor good; it is a condition of ego. You might say the fact that you all die is bad and you are welcome to say that. But it is an irrefutable fact. Your choice in the matter is how you want to deal with that fact.*

*What We are saying here is **NOT a justification** for predatory behavior, for eating without permission, whether it be economic* *exploitation, political force, moral intimidation and judgment, rape, etc. – not at all. What We are saying is that this is what you can expect from ego consciousness because it operates on the Law of Eating. This you must know if you want to effect real change in your world. This you must know if you want to begin to make different choices.*

And We are not saying that ego Eating in the emotional, intellectual and spiritual arenas is always destructive or murderous, not at all. The evolution of man's desire and need to eat on all levels is also part of what has generated the development of your great power and skill to function on the Horizontal Plane as distinct from any other life form on Earth. It generates a thirst for knowledge, for emotional input and output, for the development of stunning technologies to meet your ever-expanding survival needs. It has led to many cooperative efforts – putting your heads and your hearts together to birth something no one individual could create alone. It is responsible for the development of art, architecture, science, education, medicine, agriculture, a wide variety of cultures, spiritual pursuits, psychology, and much, much more.

*AND, at the very same time, this eating on **all** levels from one another is exactly how ego consciousness intensifies. Ego's innate sense of separateness and focus on the self also results in **an intensification of competition for resources on all those same levels, for more and better, powered by the animal instinct to Dominate to get those needs met.** You see?*

The animal instinct to compete, dominate and subdue "other" for the sake of ego's perceived need to survive and thrive not only physically but emotionally, psychologically, intellectually and spiritually (again, what you call spiritually), keeps you in constant competition for resources on all those levels. It has you eating from each other with or without consent on all those levels. And the tension in this Play of "eat and/or be eaten" keeps you scrambling not to be the one "eaten." The Law of Eating is one of the most powerful ways the dense web of Karma is created and sustained.

On the Road of Return, the road from separation back to Oneness, the Law of Eating will be illuminated and transformed. The food you eat will be taken primarily from YOUR OWN LIFE experience, not from others. The energy extracted from digesting your own experience is the energy that takes one Home to the Creator. And the eating you do, will be by consent only, and only for highest good of all.

This is White Magic.

Every time I read this, my heart pounds and my mind is flooded with the white light of Revelation. If I were reading aloud, I would stop here and just breathe with gratitude for this gift of Divine Love made manifest as the Word of God. I can think of no other way to express this.

But They did not take the slightest pause...

*Black Magic is the extreme end of the Law of Eating on an ego level. It is the attempt to eat the psychic and/or physical energy (sometimes believed to be the Soul energy) of others in an attempt, acknowledged or not, to **find immortality**. But ego will never be immortal. Only Soul is immortal. Black Magic stems from the belief that if you take the life force from another living being, that life force becomes yours and will give you limitless power on Earth and take you to your god – whatever it is you worship – or will make you a god in the flesh. **In White Magic, you use only your own energy. You take from the experience of yourself in relationship to the rest of the world.** You see, it is not just physical food that We were talking about when We told you about your world operating on the Law of Eating.*

*On the Road of Return, you eat from each other only with the CONSENT of the other and only what you need to sustain and further a Horizontal Plane existence that supports Soul to manifest through you for the highest good of all. We cannot say this often enough or loudly enough. **On the Road of***

*Return, you eat from each other only with the CONSENT of
the other and only what you need to sustain and further a
Horizontal Plane existence that supports Soul to manifest
through you for the highest good of all.* While you are in a
body, you will always need food, you will always need to connect
with others, to feel love and belonging. You will always need to
procreate, you will always be seeking new ideas, new inventions, new
understanding. This is all lawful. But on the Road of Return, you
take back all the energy you have projected out onto the Horizontal
Plane as judgment, as greed, as force — as any projection of a
Duality. You consume the energy held in that Play of Duality
within yourself and *you "ascend" on that energy alone.*

*You digest and transform all the reactions, judgments, beliefs
and feelings that keep YOU separate. This is ILLUMINATED
EATING. This is the Eating you do on the Path of Return. This
is White magic.*

You don't get to God through someone else's work or by trying to take
their energy or clinging to it. You can learn from others, but that is
not the same thing as trying to extract energy from them. Only
eat your own food. Only live on the strength of your own food. You
are the yolk of your own egg. Grow your own wings. Take your
own energy and lay it at the Guru's feet, the feet of your own Soul,
and ask that it be used for your highest good and the highest good of
all. A true Teacher will point you in this direction.

The concept of healthy boundaries in the world of psychology is
actually informed by and evidence of the impulse toward White
Magic and Planetary Return. In order to create healthy boundaries,
you have to understand what emotional, mental, sexual and spiritual
energies you are projecting onto others and what projected ego
energies you have absorbed and are absorbing. You have to build
the strength and the awareness to keep out unwanted energies and
have control over the energies you put out toward others. This focus
in the world of psychology and mental health is a great contribution
to Undoing the Laws of Gravity. White Magic emphasizes the
importance of respecting the individual integrity of self and other, to

*give and take **only** what is asked for and offered **AND ONLY** if it serves the health and well-being of both the giver and the receiver. And what serves most is the illumination of Soul, of Divine Love and Wisdom.*

The present-day concern about boundaries indicates that you are beginning to understand the impact of your projections, judgments, and blame. As a race, you are attempting to make a great departure from the original laws governing the animal kingdom. Although you have almost completely left cannibalism behind as it concerns physical eating, cannibalism is still a governing principle for humans. Emotionally you are eating each other, in some cases psychically sucking the life from each other. Economically you steal resources from others without remorse — their time, money, land, and natural resources. You are mentally and often spiritually (what you call spiritual) eating each other as well — imposing, often with horrific force, your needs, your rationales, your so-called ideologies and religious values and convictions on others, projecting blame and sin and judgment everywhere you go for the sake of some supposed gain to yourselves — money, power, righteousness. Or you idolize others and make them your god and then try to get their approval, their favor, and their love by giving yourselves away, offering yourselves up as food for them to eat. As a race on the Horizontal Plane, you are devouring each other sexually. You are raping as an addiction, as a business, as a weapon. These are the extremes of the Law of Eating as they play out on the Horizontal Plane.

This is what We call Black Magic and this is what the human race is now being called to Undo.

You tend to think of Black Magic as something only sorcerers or Darth Vaders perpetrate. But in fact, as the Sands of your evolution intensify and heat up, you see the play of Black Magic everywhere when you look at how many nations, groups and individuals unquestioningly take what does not belong to them and what is not freely given. Black Magic is not a mystery. Neither is White Magic.

WHITE MAGIC IS THE PROCESS BY WHICH YOU UNDO, *the process by which you eat ONLY the yolk inside your own shell. You eat up your own projections, your own false beliefs about self and other and the false ego beliefs that have been projected onto you that you have absorbed from others. As a result, you make room for the Light and Love of Soul to power your engine and manifest through you, where previously ego ran the show, and you begin to grow your wings. Psychology gives you a context and a process for beginning this work of Undoing. Many spiritual practices also open the door to what We are calling White Magic. We will give you the tools and the understanding that belong to the Path of Supreme Surrender.*

On the Road of Return, you transform what you EAT and the way you EAT.

The Law of Eating—absolutely fascinating and unlike anything I had ever heard.

The more I look at what causes pain, alienation and violence in human relationships, the more I see how much we eat and are eaten without consent, how much we project onto ourselves and others—individually, in families, political and religious groups, and as nations. The projections fundamentally boil down to beliefs in Good and Evil, Better and Worse. This religion is better than that one, white skin is superior to brown skin, men are superior to women, capitalism is better than socialism, thin is better than fat, rational is better than emotional, force is better than mediation or peacemaking, and on and on and on.

It is fundamental in current psychology that these projections are generally understood to arise from what we are taught in early childhood from our caregivers and from the cultures in which we are raised. For every projection we consider "Good," there will always be a corresponding projection of "Bad." This is the nature of Duality. In the field of psychology, we now understand that our unconsciously held projections are not necessarily true. We try to see where these projections come from and work to undo the hold they have on our automatic unconscious responses, so that we can choose new, healthier responses.

The impact of projection can be seen on every level of human existence. On a very small individual scale, I got the message as a child that I was the "homely" sister. With nothing and no one to counteract this message, I completely internalized it. I saw that vision of myself when I looked in the mirror. As a little girl, I prayed to God to help me survive a life I believed I would spend alone. As I grew up, I unquestioningly believed men and women alike saw me as unattractive, unappealing and therefore unlovable. And while I say this is the small scale, this one projection caused years of untold pain, fear of rejection, a constant need to withdraw, and extreme difficulty embracing myself as a woman.

In fact, what happens to us on this "small scale" is widespread, epidemic. As a psychotherapist, I see daily the enormous toll of human suffering resulting from the projections people internalize in childhood. A teacher publicly puts a student down and that child grows up believing she is stupid, perhaps idolizes those she thinks are smarter or projects the same judgment onto others in order to feel better about herself. A child is abused and he grows up believing he deserved to be beaten, or that his children deserve the same treatment. A child of color is taunted on the playground and no one defends him. He grows up believing his is unlovable, unworthy, powerless, invisible, inferior, deserving of abuse, or he picks on another minority.

I see the long-lasting, crippling, devastating effects of such internalized projections and I see those same effects passed down from generation to generation.

So, what I am talking about is not really small-scale. It is the microcosm of what we do to one another globally as a race of beings, resulting in racial and religious wars, ethnic "cleansing," extreme exploitation and abuse of the poor, of women and children, AND BLAMING OUR VICTIMS while we go on victimizing—all so that someone or some group can have more money, more power, or believe they have more righteousness. This is the extreme end, the most destructive aspect, of what They call ego Eating, Black Magic.

As discussed in Book I, *A Light in the Darkness*, all this judgment and projection fuels and is fueled by the great Duality of Domination and Submission, which is a product of the great Masculine/Feminine divide. In some form, a person must dominate another to eat without permission. And the more the Masculine assertive energies are split from the Feminine receptive, nurturing energies, within individuals and groups of individuals, the more you see extremes in Domination and Submission in human behavior. Understanding that judgment and projection are ways we "eat" and are "eaten" in the world of ego consciousness, that we are still cannibals on more levels than we imagine, is mind-blowing. It sheds enormous light on why we keep focusing outside ourselves, why we are more easily caught up in action/ reaction. It reveals the Darkness that causes so much escalating global human pain and suffering.

They tell us that we were asked and we agreed as Souls to play certain parts on the Horizontal Plane, these very parts that fuel the intense projections of Good and Evil, Love and Hate, Have and Have Not, Domination and Submission, etc., and thus create the ongoing drama of the entire Family of Man. This is what They call the Sleep of Forgetting. AND, They also tell us that we came here ultimately to remember, to undo the trance of ego and wake of from that sleep, and that we all have parts in **that Play** as well. And to play our part on the Road of Return, we learn to move out of our ego consciousness, away from ego eating of each other, and into Soul consciousness where we eat up our own experiences and only take from others with their permission and for the highest good of all. Very tall order. But just as a heart patient may be told a drastic change in diet will be required for his continued survival, we are being told that a drastic change in diet on all levels of our existence—physical, sexual, emotional, mental and spiritual—is urgently needed to heal humanity's aching heart. From Their Divine point of view, what psychology has introduced as the concept of healthy boundaries is actually related to the birth of Soul consciousness in human beings.

This revelation was for me then, and is now, supremely inspiring and profoundly hopeful. To birth a new consciousness, we have to learn to eat differently. We have to learn to get the fundamental life force energy of our transformation from *ourselves*. And this is what They came to teach us how to do.

It has taken me many years to embrace emotionally and not just intellectually, the idea that in ego consciousness there will always be both cruelty and violence, love and peaceful cooperation. I am profoundly inspired and encouraged by the understanding that there is a higher meaning and purpose underlying this human journey. But looking in the face of abject human pain and suffering, I struggled greatly back in the 90's to understand in my heart why we do such terrible things to each other, and I would be lying if I said I don't have that struggle today. But I have a place to come back to now that has its foundation in my Soul, and when the world around me looks most bleak, when man's inhumanity to man overwhelms my heart, I try to remember to breathe with What Is, focus my energy on the illumination of my Soul, and pray to be of Service from that place.

Back then in 1995, I was still very much in the midst of my dialogue with Them about all this. And so I asked —

> How did we get so far afield? Did the human race somehow get lost a long time ago? Did we lose sight of the evolutionary intent to Return? Did certain individuals choose to help bring that intention back into the forefront of consciousness? Is it those individuals or groups of individuals who will suffer persecution as long as the majority does not want to hear their message or honor their role? But then that way of thinking makes it sound like some people are better than others, some good and others bad, and I know that is not what You are saying. I really do not understand how the human race could get lost from its intent, though. Because wouldn't God know what the possibilities were for the beings God created? How could they get lost if God didn't want that? This is all very hard to understand.

*It is not that the human race got lost. It is that the **intent is to find your way Home through this Wilderness.** Different lines of beings have agreed, on a Soul level, to incarnate repeatedly into different aspects of that intent, into different parts in the Play. We realize that this is a vague statement but be patient. You, for instance, on that Soul level, agreed to be what might be called a shadow bearer. It is not that certain beings have chosen to be light bearers to remind the human race of its purpose. **The whole configuration of human interaction has required both those who call loudly to certain issues that are being worked out through experience (in an evolutionary sense) and also those who resist. And within the individual, the same opposing forces are also playing out — Soul calls, ego resists.***

*Let Us repeat — **the whole configuration of human interaction has required both those who call loudly to certain issues that are being worked out through experience and also those who resist. And within the individual, the same opposing*** *forces are also playing out—Soul calls, ego resists. The process of evolution in your world REQUIRES resistance,* just like Sand is required for the creation of the Pearl.

You all started from the same place, but certain lines of incarnation agreed to play the more aggressive, more territorial, and more sexually rigid and differentiated roles. They bring the "law of the jungle" into human civilization, as this is the part they were asked and agreed to play. They are part of the raw material, as it were, of the experiment. The experiment, you see, was to mirror the act of creation within a finite form. **There are many different lines along which different groups of Souls were asked and agreed to incarnate. These lines are related to what We call the Rays of Creation.**

This is a very big topic which opened up a huge outpouring of information about the chakras; this will be explored in depth in future books.

For now, when you ask why a Soul would choose a path of persecution, know that it is a part played in the process of Pearl formation. Those who call loudly to certain issues very often cause great irritation under the skin of the evolving human psyche, evolving human consciousness. On the ego plane of existence, this plays out with people who champion racial issues, minority rights, economic injustice, scientific discoveries that challenge existing beliefs, alternative spiritual practices, etc. Or you might see it play out in those who simply have a different hair style, play alternative music or do not adhere to some other accepted behavior or preference.

On the ego plane, the irritation caused by the voices of change or challenge to existing beliefs, on all levels, ignites Duality; it fires up judgment and the preoccupation with Good and Evil, Right and Wrong, Better and Worse. Ego will always seek to impose its values, desires, and will on others in an endless, and, from Our point of view, fruitless, struggle. But this is exactly how ego responds to diversity and perpetuates Duality and division.

*On a Soul level, that same irritation calls out for what We call Pearl formation – for the Light and Love of Soul to embrace diversity, see the Teacher **for you** in all experience rather than the right or wrong of it. You are being asked to extract the energy inherent in the irritation of differing beliefs and desires as the raw material you came here to transform into Soul consciousness and Divine Love **within yourselves**. This is Pearl formation. This is what Soul does with all that irritation under your skin.*

So often the voices of change or challenge to existing beliefs and practices are judged as wrong and heretical, and often great force is used to silence them. At the same time, the nature of ego consciousness is to "eat" continually on every level, and the tension between opposing beliefs, desires and behaviors also creates and continues to create the very resistance against which we have evolved great advances in human understanding, functioning and mechanisms for survival. AND, in the process, many people are revered and many people are alienated, hated, persecuted and killed. This is a part of what They call Sand, the irritation of opposition that makes up our Horizontal or ego plane existence. And in this great Play, we were all asked and we all agreed, They say, to play these differing parts. The astounding beauty and power of Their Wisdom is that They have come to teach us how to undo this powerful trance of ego so that we can now begin play our **Soul** parts on the Road of Return, the Road Home. These are parts that are not in opposition to anything or anyone. They are parts in which we stand for and express Soul's Divine Love and Wisdom within the lives we are now living, within the relationships, talents, circumstances and difficulties into which we were born.

If you look at the entire evolutionary development of the human race, you will see that something is being forged here out of the raw material that human beings represent, just as you humans forge something not found in nature out of natural elements. And that *forging process often involves intense fire and heat. We have a lot more to say about Fire, but for now, We want to say that one element of the raw material that is being used here is the underlying animal nature of the human race and that is why We remind you that you are animals operating under the laws that govern that kingdom. Animals are wired to survive physically. To that end, they eat physical food and do their utmost to avoid predators. You humans, because you are hard-wired in your ego nature to eat on **all** levels, including what you understand to be a spiritual level, strive not only to prolong physical life and well-being as long as possible, but you also strive for immortality. In your emotional and intellectual nature as well, you can conceive of an existence before and after death. But know that, in essence, the striving for immortality comes from a felt memory of your essential Soul nature, a felt memory of where you really come from and the place in consciousness to which you will return.*

*On a purely ego level, this striving for immortality can only be played out in the arena of Duality. And that is why you have religious wars and people hating and condemning and murdering each other in the name of their perceived connection to God and striving for immortality. This is what the extremes of ego consciousness and Duality produce. Of course, there are also many people, even in ego consciousness, who identify with the Love aspect of their connection to Soul and their immortal nature, but in ego consciousness you will always have **both** responses because of the Law of Duality. As you learn to Eat consciously, as you practice White Magic, the whole play of ego consciousness will be illuminated, and in that Light, the Darkness will be revealed for what it is and it will lose its power. As yet, there is a long way to go.*

*But for the moment, let Us say that it is not that the human race has gone haywire and forgotten the blueprint, and is therefore about to destroy itself because it is bad or because it sinned, although it would be easy to have that interpretation. **The challenge the human race took on was to learn to consciously participate in bringing back together all the ways energy has been split into different forms.** Evolutionarily, you are moving toward an* *extreme end of the continuum of separation. You are working with something like a jigsaw puzzle spilled from the box, the original picture lost or forgotten, and there can be both a tremendous feeling of overwhelm at trying to put it back together and also great excitement and curiosity about what will emerge.*

***

This was all completely new to me. I am still stunned by the wisdom of these words and the profound and urgent need on the part of the human race to understand the Law of Eating today. Never before has our ability to dominate others in order to get our perceived needs met escalated to the point where we have the power to destroy all life as we know it. Never before have we had to face, as a race of beings, that Earth's supply is NOT endless, and that eating without immediate regard for the hand that feeds us is simply not sustainable.

We have never had to face this before, and like the classic addict, we don't want to. *I* don't want to, not when it threatens my comfort zone. But never before have our children and our children's children been at such great risk on a global level. ALL OUR CHILDREN—not some far off generation we can put out of our minds. The time is past where we can safely imagine that someday someone somewhere will figure out a solution long after we are dead.

On a very personal level, if ever there were a concept that might have transformed my early life, and IS transforming my present life, it is this one. When I was young, I turned to others constantly to accept me, see me, and show me how to be more lovable and loved. I tried to please, shine, ingratiate myself. I can still feel what it was like to pull on the psyches and emotions of others in this way, how awful it felt, how much it did not produce the desired result, and yet how relentless the drive was to "eat" in this way. What I was doing is not wrong or bad; it is very human. Biologically it is part of survival to be connected to the pack. Psychologically it is normal, understandable, and predictable to look outside oneself for validation and acceptance because we are born dependent on others for *all* our survival needs. And when early relationships are insecure, hurtful, and unsafe, the drive to "eat" the energy of others is intensified.

This "eating" takes many forms. Sometimes it looks like being overly pleasing or co-dependent, projecting a positive quality or a need onto someone and then trying to take that positive quality back from them. But often it takes the form of aggression—I'll get power or food (energy) from dominating or hurting you, making you feel the powerlessness or pain I don't want to feel. Or I'll get my sense of importance and purpose, which often turns into righteousness, from ignoring you, rejecting you and judging you so that I can feel better about myself. This eating can take the form of one group persecuting a whole segment of society it deems inferior, or it might look like me silently criticizing the lady in the grocery store with blue hair. I know this side of eating, too, as I would guess most of us do.

The ego eating I did from others never filled the void I thought it would fill. Of course, it feels good when I am accepted or someone likes me. I think as a human being it will always feel better to be loved and valued rather than hated and rejected. As a human being I will generally move toward love. At the same time, I also recognize those moments in which I have felt an illusory and fleeting sense of power from judging others. And as an ego, I know I will continue to seek my food from both sides of the spectrum, no matter how subtly I do it. My work is to catch that tendency and transform it when I can.

If I take my own personal experiences of projection and eating from others, and I magnify those energies a million or a billion times, the magnitude of how the Law of Eating plays out in our families, communities, nations, political, economic and religious groups, becomes horrifyingly clear. The extremes of eating They call Black Magic are everywhere. I understand now how we have arrived at this critical place in human evolution. We are "eating" from each other and from the Earth as never before — so often without permission and without an awareness of or regard for our impact or for the highest good of all.

Astronomical growth in human population combined with, or resulting from, record breaking advances in technology, in a world more or less run by ego consciousness, brings us to the critical place where, if we don't examine what we are eating and where we are getting our food, we will, most likely, literally die out. And like the animals we are, most of us, when faced with diminishing supply, would rather eat than be eaten. I get it.

Whether we are talking about how I criticized the lady with blue hair, didn't recycle everything I could, or got aggravated with my husband when I had to repeat myself, OR if we are talking about widespread unregulated pollution, the destruction of rainforests, the decimation of countless animal and plant species and the atmosphere itself, or if we are talking about raping women and children for profit or as a strategy of repression, invading other countries, overturning their governments and slaughtering their people to gain access to natural resources that don't belong to us, or blaming and persecuting minorities as a supposed solution to economic and cultural problems or as a justification for unrestrained power and greed — it is ALL EATING WITHOUT CONSENT from the point of view of the Divine.

From the microcosm of what I do in my own personal life to the macrocosm of what we do as an entire species, it is all Black Magic; it is all a form of trying to extract the energies of others by force for the perceived gain of enhancing and prolonging one's OWN life, whether one is an individual, a country, a race or a political or religious group. The macrocosm reflects the microcosm. It makes a difference to the planet that I can learn to eat in this new way myself. This is what my Soul came here to do.

If ever there was a time in human history when we need to understand the power of the Law of Eating, it is now. The less we have, the hungrier we are. Millions of people around the globe are experiencing extraordinarily high levels of physical, emotional, mental and spiritual poverty, discrimination, hurt at human hands and an extreme lack of safety. These conditions intensify the need to "eat" the energies of others on all levels of survival and that keeps the cycle going. If ever there was a time in human history when there is an urgent need to make a radical change in our eating habits, to understand enlightened Eating, it is now. If ever there was a time for White Magic to transform our world and save us, literally, it is now.

They came to teach us White Magic.

Chapter 9

The Experiment

*T*he human race is being pushed along the course of its evolutionary path just as you personally are being pushed. It does not matter to God if this experiment is what you might call a success or failure because those words do not exist in God's vocabulary. But it matters to man, and it should, because that is a part of what mankind is working on and literally, your lives depend on it.*

When the human race creates something as destructive to the life of the planet as a Holocaust, as the atom bomb, as chemicals that destroy the environment you depend on for your survival, the meaning of that from a planetary perspective is that the human race is asking to be pushed hard along its evolutionary Path because it has raised the stakes just about as high as they can go, just like you individually take on bigger and bigger challenges for the sake of your own growth or why some have to hit bottom in order to heal.

This is the experiment that the human race asked to participate in. There was a Divine Impulse or Intention to create an incarnate being of the animal world that could mirror in microcosm the act of Creation in a particular way. Something, very roughly, like God creating a toy god, just as you as human beings make dolls in your own image, and now robots that can perform more complex human functions. **God took the raw material of formless being and created worlds and creatures and states of being from formlessness. The human race was asked and agreed to experience the Sleep of Forgetting the Source, to descend** *into ego consciousness, as the raw material from which, eventually, to create Soul consciousness.* A creature of the animal kingdom was chosen because it has the power of movement and of manipulation of objects already inherent in its nature.

It is **not an accident** that mankind has been able to develop all the capacities for creation and destruction that he now exhibits. It is not a random force of evolution at work here. The **intent** behind the Path of the evolution of human beings is **what has determined and will continue to determine** the development of the human brain and body structure, as well as man's physical and technological power to impact the environment. It was the **intent** of Oneness that human beings develop sophisticated mental, emotional, physical and social capabilities in order to become the vehicle for Soul consciousness. Such things as computer science and telecommunications, aeronautics and advanced medicine, space exploration, exploration of the psyche, and in the present day – exploration of all the interconnections between body and energy and the "whole" in which the parts exist on all possible levels– all are manifestations of that intent.

Man can now move things without touching them directly, he can see into areas far beyond the range of ordinary vision, he can talk to someone on the other side of the world or someone beyond the atmosphere of Earth, he can graft a part of one body onto another and research the atomic level of cell structure. He can create exquisite hybrids of natural plants, witness the birth of a star," and "save" a life. AND mankind can **destroy** in equal proportion to his ability to **create**. He can kill hundreds of thousands of creatures – plants, animals and microorganisms – all at once with weapons and poisons and chain saws. He can destroy the atmosphere around the Earth, and he can destroy his world as he knows it altogether. Do these abilities not begin to mirror in miniature some of the powers of the Creator? Nothing is an accident. None of these developments is accidental.

Man's ability to produce airplanes and rockets and other vehicles that travel in space, and which have to be more powerful than *the physical force of gravity in order to leave the Earth's gravitational pull, is a testimony to the direction that he is intended to take in the areas of intellect and emotion and spirit. He is intended to* **leave Gravity***.*

What We are saying is that mankind has not yet linked his power with his spirit. This is the work of the human race at this time. This is exactly the same challenge and the same evolutionary leap you are facing as an individual—not only to find and release and strengthen your individual power, but also to link it with your Soul's intent for you. *That is the endgame from Our perspective. The human race has come to the end of the line with its power to destroy, though you certainly may go on to develop weapons more lethal than those you now have. But when your greatest power on that level has become the instrument of your own extinction — and it HAS — you have come to the end of that particular road, whether as a race you know it or not.*

What will it take for the human race **as a whole** *to change courses? Think of how much how much time, energy and determination you now pour into all your technologies both destructive and constructive. What if the same amount of energy were being channeled into an effort to enter the mind of God? Imagine if the same time, energy and determination now being focused on racial discrimination and ethnic "cleansing," massive accumulation of wealth, influence and control, were being channeled into an effort to enter the* **heart** *of God?*

Chapter 10

Soul Parts

The deeper I went, the more profound and universal the messages became, the more I doubted myself. You would think I might have felt only joy and gratitude at being visited by a presence so Divinely loving and wise. And of course, I did feel those things, deeply, tearfully and with great awe. But I also felt like the lowliest worm, the strangest of all creatures, and even more of a misfit. I simply could not grasp who I was or how I could possibly be the vehicle for such Divine Wisdom. If T had not been there to affirm my reality, I might have believed I was truly crazy. In fact, if T had not been there, I most likely would not have been able to go on. That was the part he played for me, and I was then and am today so grateful for that as well.

I am plagued by the fear that You will abandon me. It becomes harder and harder to write. I am so convinced I am just not worthy and You will leave me.

We do not leave you. Fear urges you to leave Us. The test for you is not to deny Us, even when the mind of your personality is overwhelmed. God never leaves you.

Remember this: Nothing stays the same except God and the Living Truth. The essence is changeless and all else is in constant flux. Do not try to hold onto anything. Do not try to carve a new identity for yourself. Do not try to create a new *picture of who you are. Rather, keep letting go of **what you thought you were**. Can you see the distinction? When a Divine flood washes over you, swim in it without holding onto anything, old or new. You can do it. It will seem to take everything you have, but do it. Surrender to the Unknown. There have been many lifetimes where you came to a point like this and gave up. You went into craziness, confusion and fear. This time you asked not to repeat that pattern. We see and understand how difficult that pattern is to transcend. Why do you think We are here as strongly as We are?*

> I just need to know—am I using all this simply to alleviate my aloneness, my fears that I am nothing, not really a good therapist, certainly not a psychic, not even happy, just someone who can't quite make it work and who is very imaginative and clever at re-representing all that to herself? This fear is very powerful.

*No one said this would be an easy lifetime for you, darling. It is anything but that. Our answer to you is that nothing matters in this lifetime except the constant challenge to listen to the call of Soul, to stay with Self and not abandon Self, NO MATTER WHAT THE FIRE. Do you think the Fire will burn less hot because We are here or because you are a good person or because you have struggled so hard or for so long already? **The Fire burns hot because you asked to clear the Path for Return.***

*This life is about **integrating** all the Soul Parts of yourself that died unintegrated. We give you the Map but you must walk the terrain. Doesn't it make sense that there will be a certain ecstasy in receiving the Map and a lot of discomfort when your feet actually get blistered on the road?*

Let go of all images of yourself. Pray and walk and meditate and write and chant and go out there and burn and burn. We will always be here. You are on a holy road. And when you lose sight of that because you have fallen into an old abyss that once buried you, know that experience for what it is. You have died in despair and hopelessness over and over again and so you fall into those same places easily now. Laying yourself at the Master's feet means you are willing to see those pitfalls for what they are, and you are willing to climb out NOW, no matter what it takes.

The reason you are given information about past lives is so that you can see the PATTERN of experience your Soul has chosen to transform, AND to integrate all the Soul Parts that have been split off in the process of incarnation over and over again. That is the highest purpose of past life work. *Whether you see a lifetime of persecution or one in which you had a direct connection to Earth Spirits or you were a nameless slave, it is all for the same purpose. With each incarnation, parts of the psychic experience are split off, left behind, spread out over the Horizontal Plane for the purpose of "seeding" ego experience for yourself and for all those with whom you travel. The reason why you are shown the way you died in past lives is because the state of consciousness at death is a representation of the unintegrated energies you carry with you into following lives. When you are on the Road of Return, these split off Soul Parts,* **these split off aspects of the experience Soul took on to Redeem for the Creator,** *are presented to you one way or another. Past life work is one way to access these energies that call out to be integrated.*

I knew I had a lot of work of integration to do. Everything that was said made perfect sense. As a result of the witch lifetime alone, I could see why I was plagued with doubt, why I feared persecution, and why it would be easier to believe I had gone crazy. That "perfect sense" made it all sound like it should be easy. Just bring those darn parts back together! If you died countless deaths not trusting yourself, losing your faith, if you gave in to the intense projected energies of others and could not hold your ground—well then, just don't do that anymore!! If you had strengths and abilities in the past, just access them now! In my mind, it seemed clear. In my feelings, I knew that the psychic hold of those terrified unintegrated parts had tremendous power, **and I was finally**

beginning to understand that the power they had over me was exactly what I came here to transform into Soul consciousness. It felt clear, it felt right... and it felt enormous.

I had to go back into the Fire where so many Soul Parts had been left. I thought immediately of the Burning Bush in the Bible, the miracle Moses saw leaving Egypt on his way to the Promised Land. I suddenly knew what that image meant. It symbolized standing in one's Fires *without* being burned. Perhaps Moses was being given a sign of how to walk through the Fires he would face. But it's one thing to *talk* about standing in your Fires unscathed. It's quite another when you *actually feel the flames*, when you see your beautiful daughter's eyes dilated, when you barely recognize her, when you see her flushing her exquisite life force down the toilet. That Fire is hot. You don't want to stand in it for one f--ing second! But you have to learn how to do it all the same. You know you came here to *do exactly that* and you *want* to do it, you really do. Well, actually, there's still a good bit of you that just wants the Fire to go away. But that doesn't appear to be one of the options.

> You said again that the hurting one inside me, the one so terrified to speak, is still surrounded by dark energies from the past. I saw You just reach out a hand toward her and You said, *Take Our hand* and she reached out to You. You said to put her in the center of the Cross and show her that the past is over. At that moment, she was a mass of blackened ashes. You said the past was over, and those ashes were now a symbol of trans-formation. You said that even in nature when lightning strikes the ground and burns whole forests, it is for the good. It rejuvenates the Earth and new life springs from the richness of the burnt soil. You said, *Be like that, be rich like burnt soil and produce new growth.* And that felt good.

I wanted to be like that in the worst way, but that time had not yet come.

> ... Yesterday the feeling of loneliness and anxiety turning to panic was terrible. No matter how much Your light pours in, I keep returning to this place. Hell couldn't be much worse. It was so bad I was in physical pain. So, somewhere in the early evening, I sat in my kitchen and talked to You out loud and I told You I was willing to stand in this Fire consciously, and that I wouldn't fight it anymore. I said I would pass the negative judgments about myself through the Cross, breathe with them and let them pass out. I said I was willing to feel the pain of loneliness. I said I accept that this is absolutely meant to be and that it is for my highest good.
>
> This was one of very few times that I actually totally faced this feeling. Very soon the feelings were completely gone and I came back to "normal." I wish I had a way to describe how absolutely insane I feel at these times. I go out into a place where there is no connection to anything and I believe there is no way back. Now I see that there is a way back and the way back is *through*, and I can do it and You are there to help me if I just call on You. I see that the **final step of passing the feelings through the Cross is consciously letting Your Love in as the dark passes out.**

*You have to work with the ego level as you seek to move to the Vertical Plane. There is no way around that. Understand now that what you call the child in you is also much more than that. Not only is the inner child the psychic embodiment of all the unresolved aspects of your incarnate path through lifetimes, **it is also a microcosm of the Part you agreed to play in the course of human evolution.** So you see, this identity goes way beyond one lifetime.*

This is why the experience of the man in the campground was so powerful — because as you open the door to the energies of Return, the unintegrated aspects of your super-psyche (your psyche as it exists as a conglomerate of all past life experience) will make themselves known one way or another so that they can all be integrated and transformed. Therefore, you can see that inner child work is a doorway, from Our point of view, into **the Path of Return because it is the inner child that holds the pattern of the Soul's entire journey in form.**

So, what They call Soul Parts are really unresolved and unintegrated aspects of past life experience in many different personalities. I'm not sure why They use the term Soul Parts as these seem to be unresolved aspects of ego experience, but that is the term They use. These parts are the exact equivalent of what we call inner child parts in present day psychology. Inner child parts embody the formative experiences, beliefs, coping mechanisms and views of self and other that run our lives. People come to therapy when these inner child parts are injured in some way that negatively affects their present-day functioning. This Divine explanation of Soul Parts, unintegrated and unresolved aspects of all past life experiences, vastly expands the concept of the inner child to include our entire experience of incarnation in human form. This concept is a pivotal bridge between the world of psychology and the world of Soul. All pain, They say, is Soul calling you Home. The unresolved pain of the inner child can suddenly be understood as a gateway to God, just as it was for me on that remarkable day in 1994. My journey down into the painful past *in this life* opened the door to the Soul Parts that held the same patterns of experience, beliefs and coping mechanisms carried over from past lives. *And* as a result, the door was also opened to lifetimes of buried strengths, and to Soul Parts like Talking Flower that held energies already redeemed, already freed from the weight of ego conscious-ness. Thus, my journey down into the abyss opened the door to Return.

The inner child in you holds **the keys to every hook, every trigger and every attachment you still have, to every area of your existence where Gravity still holds you down. She is your food. Everything that must be "eaten" and digested and transformed is contained in her.** *That is why you saw the vision of yourself as a living temple, why you were told to worship yourself, bow down to yourself. In the world of Duality, it is so easy to believe you should be something other than what you are. On the Path of Return, you are the exact food you came to consume for the journey Home. You see, don't you, that what is unfolding as events in your life, as issues with yourself and with others and incidences or coincidences that occur daily — these are the food your Soul is eating.*

So now you ask about why you are alone, why you have no husband to come home to and share your life with? Why you have been alone so long, why everyone else you know has someone? The answer is that you are eating the energy of your aloneness in this sense and when you are done eating it in this way, when you have extracted and digested every bit of the Soul food your Soul requires, then you will be done with this experience. There is nothing here that can be compared to any other person. Someone who is working with other issues may be extremely envious of your motherhood just as you are envious of their relationship. All of that is not the point. See the uselessness and inaccuracy of the projection here and take it back. Transform that energy at every turn of the road. Bow down to yourself in everything. Surrender to yourself, to the wisdom and perfection of your own Soul. Do nothing but breathe with the Guru, who lives and breathes inside you, and everything you need will come to you. And, as We said, it may not come in the form you imagine.

I was able to have a very simple and lovely evening. I lit candles and put on a chant and folded laundry and petted my animals and it was wonderful. Remembering what You told me when I was out in the garden today.

Let Us say something about breathing and air. Breathing is the process and air is the food. When you breathe with the Guru, you actually extract from the air physical properties and energies not available through ordinary breathing. Do you know that consciousness "acts" on matter? This is a truth of physical reality. Therefore, when you breathe with God, with the Teacher within, you actually fan the Fires of your own evolution. You move into greater consciousness of the Plan, greater consciousness of self as a vehicle, and greater conscious intention, agreement and desire to participate. In this round, Fire lights up many past lives for you so that you can die consciously now to what killed you in the past. This phase will not last forever.

As We said before, when you breathe with Us and listen with God in your heart, you intensify and speed up your process along your Path, and you will also connect to all avenues of truth necessary for you. With each door that opens, the Horizontal Plane energies that are yours to Redeem for the Creator will be thrown into the Fire so that the Light of Soul can shine from you.

I was breathing with Them, and with the Plant World and the Water World the best I could, and the energies that I apparently came to Redeem went directly into that Fire, the magnitude of which I could not possibly have imagined.

Chapter 11

A Fiery Distillation

You were telling me that when you have reached a certain point in the buildup of Karmic experience over lifetimes, you come to a place where everything of significance in your whole course of incarnation over centuries, comes with you into one lifetime, almost as a distillation of the essence of your deepest challenges and commitment to work through those challenges. You said that in that lifetime, which is a great and blessed opportunity, you meet everyone and everything of essential significance to your Path. What I heard You say was that the central players in that drama will closely resemble the exact players you met before.

This explained why the people in my witch lifetime were almost all people I know and am close to in the present. What was amazing was that I *recognized* them. They had totally different faces but I *recognized* them immediately!

What is equally amazing is that at that time I had absolutely no experience with retrieving past lives. I was incredulous that I recognized the players in my witch lifetime instantly and without a shadow of a doubt. But I had no idea then that this seems to be what many people experience when they recall past lives. In recent years, I have read many accounts of other people's past life memories, and in every case, they recognized the players in past lives as some of the central players in their present lives. This has given me an added external source of validation of my experience. At the time, however, I was completely unaware of this.

> I knew that the person I had not yet seen was my father. I said I wasn't ready to see my father and I wanted to keep it that way, but I had an instantaneous flash of a man in a round black hat with a wide brim with a very flat, low top and the word "beadle" was very strongly in my mind. The doubt of what I have been seeing is beginning to go away. There was no time for imagination and besides that, I consciously did not want a picture.

And so, my conscious mind came in immediately and stopped whatever was trying to emerge. I couldn't stay with it.

You are experiencing the blessed opportunity to recapitulate lifetimes in this one life. **To burn consciously now means to burn away all unconsciousness of the presence and the love of God and to participate in the manifestation of Divine Love on Earth.**

> And still, I just go in and out of utter disconnection and panic. I would think that the severity of the pain and the fact that I have had it for as long as I can remember would finally convince me that *something* must have happened to create terror of this magnitude. But not only do I suffer with these feelings, I still do not fully believe or trust myself. It's still so automatic to think I am crazy.

Phyllis, **this is your Cross.** *This is what you carry up your particular mountain. Hold out your arms and see yourself* **on** *this Cross. See Jesus as your Teacher and your model for the true meaning of the Cross. Jesus was nailed up on the Cross of the lack of true belief in and understanding of God that was a part of his times, not his own lack of belief. He was willing to die in the way he did to make the message real for those who could hear it –* **that on your true Cross, you do not die. You are reborn.** *Many people like to think* *of that as the resurrection of the body itself, but that is not what this is about.* **You are reborn into Soul Consciousness, into God consciousness, in which there is no such thing as Death. This is the true meaning of Everlasting Life.**

You, Phyllis, are nailed up on the Cross of a lack of belief in yourself, and you will stay there, unfortunately, and you will suffer as long as you deny yourself. You don't need a stake and a trial in this life. You are your own internalized judge and jury of the Inquisition. You burn yourself at the stake over and over again.

Now, sit here with Us, and tell Us exactly what you see inside. Tell Us everything you see and feel and know and intuit. Everything.

My mouth aches. I want to cry but I can't. My jaw is very tight like I am trying to keep it shut. My chest is also aching and the pain in my heart is indescribable but if I could put any words to it at all it would be like death, like I don't want to be alive and feel what I feel. Like all good feeling of life is gone. There is only emptiness and pain and a blank mind. The most intense feelings are definitely in my mouth and jaw. It feels like some of that energy is about not talking and not expressing anything. Not even like I am conscious of wanting to talk and can't, but more like I just never could. This is so real. I'm crying at how much I've blocked this out.

Are these feelings true? Is there anything here you have made up?

No.

Do you understand why We ask you that?

Yes, because I don't ever totally want to believe this and when I do, I manage to erase it later.

*Yes. **And that is what you do with Us also**. You erase Us. Do you see why you have to do this work? Do you see that this is your Cross? It is this—**It is carrying a truth that you yourself fear and at the same time want desperately to proclaim. This is your Cross.***

*It is the theme of your life as a witch. You came into this life with the need to speak and the equally powerful need to hide—even from yourself. You think hiding keeps you safe. As a personality, you came in prepared to split off from your truth. As a Soul, you came to heal that split. But the memory of that lifetime itself is not as important as you think. **Believing** what is already there is the bridge you have not fully crossed. If you believed, fully and completely, what you felt in your body just now, you would actually be on the road out of this hell. You wouldn't have to worry about feeling crazy.*

Do you know what craziness is? Craziness is what overcomes a person when he cannot bear his own truth. People go crazy in wars or catastrophes or in abuse situations when they can't bear the pain and they go "out" into some safer, distanced or split off place inside their own mind. Or they go crazy because even if they have been able to bear the pain, they cannot tolerate having no one to tell or having no one believe them. You have been kind of crazy in that sense, not in the sense you have believed, which is that you believed you made things up that weren't true because you were born with a screw loose.

People are not born with a screw loose, no matter what anyone thinks. Some people are born with organic deficiencies or anomalies that actually skew their perception of the world compared to the general population, but that is not what We are talking about and that is not you.

You notice that the terrible feelings you were having a little while ago are gone, don't you? See that you cannot be relieved of something that did not exist in the first place. You couldn't feel better if the work you just did was irrelevant to the cause.

I have not been able to find any kind of peace all my life because of these feelings.

Yes, We know that.

I think I am amazed that You are still here.

…The feelings in my throat and mouth are again intense. I don't want to go there so badly but there is nothing else to do.

Just write down everything you feel, let anything that is there come into your consciousness.

It's the same feeling, of pressure on my neck, like I'm going to choke and die and that my life force is hovering right around my mouth and throat and is stuck there, and it can't quite get back into my body. Maybe it is a psychic fact that a piece of my spirit is still hovering outside and maybe it literally comes back to haunt me, to let me know it is there. What needs to happen with this piece of my spirit?

Breathe and swallow. Your breathing almost stops when this feeling comes on and then it is only very shallow. The muscles in your mouth and jaw are tight. When you breathe in and swallow deeply and consciously, you are giving the message to this still split-off part of you that it has permission to re-enter. So, do it now. Bow down to this now. Say to yourself, "God dwells within this, within every aspect of my being." Bring God into this feeling. Breathe God into your mouth and your throat. Swallow God. Say to yourself, "There is no place in me God cannot go."

Swallowing is the hardest. My throat feels so small and tight. I don't know what this is about…

Later…As I was lying in the bathtub, I was thinking that this would be the place where I would walk away. Where my own inner world, still filled with this mysterious pain and nausea would darken Your door and I would believe it was shut and walk away. I realize that You are right. It isn't You who would leave me but the other way around. Knowing that is comforting in a way. Whatever this truth is that is waiting for me is the very thing that would make me turn my back on You. So, this morning I made a promise to myself that I won't do that. And maybe I'm in a doom and gloom mode right now, but I think it is going to get even harder.

What We wanted to say to you is that Our coming to you in the ways We have been and will continue to do, are only a piece of what this is all about. There is a real road you must walk. We cannot walk the Path for you but you cannot walk the Path without Us. This is the point where you have left Us in the past, but not through fault. You went as far as you were intended to go in past lifetimes. Of course, you are frightened now. Let Us be here. This is a rough part of the road, We have no argument with that, but you can walk it. We can walk it together. Don't let go of Us.

There is nowhere to go, nowhere to run. I have a terrible headache.

Read the headache.

The whole top of my head hurts and down the sides to the back of my jaw. My forehead hurts. There is a tremendous block in my head. There is something I don't want to let in but I don't know what it is, and there are intense feelings behind the block.

The headache is energy that has become rigidified over a long period of time. It is how you try to make your body impenetrable to the feelings you are having. The body tries to block sensation by blocking energy flow. These energy blocks often manifest later in life as illness.

And then it comes. I don't ask for it. It just comes, like a volcano erupting after weeks of tremors waking me in the night.

> I see her, a little girl, maybe ten years old, in a long gray dress. The beadle is holding her by the arms. He's taking her to a stake! Her screams are lodged in my head like daggers in the back of a skull... *They are going to burn a child!*
>
> Oh God, I have been looking for her, trying to save her all my life. Is that why I have been so drawn to working with children? But I couldn't save her and likewise in this life, I became absolutely paralyzed in the face of danger to a child or threat to a child or the cries of a child. Oh, I see it all. Thoughts of my father come into this but I can't stay with them.

Just stay with the headache. Strange as this may sound, see it as a blessing, see it as a gift.

> I see him. I see the beadle. He is leading the little girl to some point near the stake. Then someone else grabs her. He does nothing to stop them. I'm screaming, "She is only a child!" I lock my eyes onto his but he looks straight ahead. His eyes are frozen over, his body rigid. He moves on and away. I can't see him anymore. He is my only hope! I want to die, but death is not enough. I want to have never been born. God, take away this whole life! Make me never have been!
>
> The beadle's eyes, I know them in this life. Not quite the same. Sad, but maybe sealed over, too. That is my main feeling about my father, this sense of an underlying sadness or fear of something.

There is no way I will ever be able to describe how **real** all of this felt, as if it were truly happening in the present—with exactly the same quality of trauma in my body and my emotions as the unearthed memories from this life. I was absolutely unable to go further on my own. I called T and did an extra session that evening. I wrote about it the next morning.

> I went back to the scene of the little girl being taken to the stake. The agony was overwhelming—lifetimes of persecution searing through my body. You said, *"Open your eyes and look at them,"* and the psychic and physical pain was beyond description. I felt like I was actually back there. I could see them.
>
> I bite down very hard. Pain shoots through my head. I see smoke.
>
> After that I moved into my connection to Soul and to You and out of my body and away from the stupidity and blindness and destructive perversity of these people. All the body sensations died down. I looked at them and left them to their own Souls and their own lessons and blessed them but disconnected myself from them. You said these people are the same people in my life now. It was astounding to realize how deeply connected I am to the people who have hurt me, how much I still want them to love me, accept me, see me and hear me, and how much I lov them.
>
> The statement that came up again and again from You was, *"If it is a choice between abandoning them and abandoning yourself, abandon them!"* This is a theme of many of my relationships in this lifetime, that I still desperately want love from people who can't love me. I am just beginning to grasp all this.

When I woke up this morning, the first thing I said to myself was, "I'm okay today." It was such a relief. I know it is not the point to just feel better, but after four days of intense pain, it still feels awfully good not to be in the pit of it today.

At the time of your death in the witch lifetime, you were not able to perceive Our presence, though We were truly there with you. The fear and judgment being screeched at you and the pain of believing that you had hurt all those you loved and who loved you, by not recanting, by simply knowing what you knew and sharing what you knew, and the pain of that terrible death itself combined with the simultaneous death of the child who was burned along with you — all combined (and understandably so) to overwhelm you at the end so that you were not able to hold the sense of Our Reality or Our presence. That is the state in which you died. The imprint of overwhelming loss, abandonment and pain was enormous. It has stayed with you and is, in essence, what you are experiencing now on a daily basis. So strong is the imprint, you continually believe you have been or will be abandoned and destroyed. This psychic imprint from the witch lifetime is one example of what We are calling a Soul Part — unresolved ego energy from a past life.

*In this lifetime, you have the opportunity to consciously Undo every obstacle to Return **that you had agreed to take on** from the beginning. This is what We mean when We say that a person will meet a lifetime that recapitulates their entire incarnate path. All people will do this at one point or another. This is your point. The witch lifetime was indeed a climax lifetime in the sense of the full and final condensation of all that energy of Destruction into its most potent form on the Horizontal Plane of experience for you.*

*You **chose** to come back with these people but not for the reasons you thought, not to get their love and acceptance this time, but to become free of whatever they were projecting onto you and you onto them. We are happy for you that you went through this the way you did. You will see light at the end of this tunnel. No accident that you have so often said, "I feel like I'm burning." Wash your* *feet with cool water with the knowledge that they are holy, that they stand now in the flames of your Resurrection and they do not burn. Stand on your Cross and consciously direct all the dark energy of that lifetime through yourself on the Cross and into Soul, to be used by Soul for your highest good. We are with you.*

It was undeniable that this agonizing past life memory had as real and devastating an impact on my thoughts, feelings, body, beliefs, and behaviors as anything that had happened in this present life. Awareness of the reality of the Circle of my own Incarnations was bursting through the tight wall of my limited personality, revealing itself to me and helping me solve the mystery of myself. My own Soul parts were begging for integration.

It had taken me 48 years to be able to sit quietly with myself and simply breathe. And here I was, at last... just barely breathing.

I feel so eternally grateful for Your presence.

We are here for you and for God and that is all. We are servants only.

***

Need I say more about The Law of Eating, the Duality of Domination and Submission, Black Magic? A woman speaks of an experience of Jesus to the Church, and is burned alive. Massive projections of judgment onto the Feminine — projections of shame, inferiority, presumption, and I daresay jealousy — culminating in the attempt to take the life of the Feminine itself (and perhaps attempting to take her Soul as well) with brutal force. All to feed illusions of righteousness, power, and control. This, my Divine Voice says, is at the core of human suffering today, the great

Masculine/Feminine divide escalating into rampant rape and murder of the Feminine, of woman, mother of life for male and female alike—and rape and murder of Earth, mother of life for us all.

Chapter 12

Hitting Bottom

I went out and walked my dog. I was very aware of my breathing and I kept saying Your words to myself — I am not afraid, I get out of the way, and I trust. I felt the energy moving through my heart as I always do when I breathe through the Cross.

And just as I was getting home, I thought again of the information I got quite a while back which said that my very last life before the present one was a life in Nazi Germany in which I died in a concentration camp as a child of about seven. Why did I need to come back and do it again after the witch lifetime?

*This was a different type of lifetime for you and for thousands of others like you. You see, you **chose**, while out of body, to be one of those to go through the Nazi extermination experience. The difference between that lifetime and this one is that you incarnated to serve with your body primarily. That is, as the child you were in that lifetime, there was no particular consciousness of what was unfolding on the Earth plane. You had no particular voice in any of it, no personal message of your own to impart. Your message was quite purely in the role you played as a body, as a Jew, as an innocent child among millions of innocents.*

On a Soul level, you/We, were quite aware of the meaning, purpose, and outcome of what was taking place on the Earth plane. You offered yourself for this experience and you simply went down to Earth as it were and played the part. This was the important dynamic in that life and that is why when you are now processing the obstacles to your Return, this life does not play a major part.

Why did I agree to do this and what exactly was I agreeing to do?

You had agreed to be a part of an experience that was about to unfold, this mass torture and attempted extermination of a race, as part of a larger process occurring on Earth. Which was, in part, that...

Okay, I find myself very frightened to go on. How can I possibly understand or accept some larger truth that all that horrific torture and murder and hatred was for a purpose? How can I imagine that the brutal murder of innocent adults, children and babies was for a purpose or that it is today, because genocide is still happening, murder and torture and persecution are still happening? I **can't** grasp it on any scale. I want to stop writing. And even if I were to "get it," this feels like something I couldn't possibly speak out loud, that it would make people angry and possibly hate me or that it would minimize the horror of what happened because we "chose" it? At the same time, I am listening that this comes from You, I feel I have no choice but to write Your words.

First of all, Phyllis, you do have a choice here. If you truly want to get up and not touch this issue, you may. However, you will remember that you asked and that is why We attempted to answer.

I know, and I don't really want to close myself off. I just want to acknowledge the feeling.

*Understandable. But you see, We also want to illustrate for you again, that in this lifetime you have the opportunity to **choose**, without being under the shadow of extreme duress, but out of Love of Self and God, **to participate**. This is so important for you to recognize and absorb into your whole being. **It is a spiritual*** *paradox that you have the opportunity to choose on the* *Earth plane that which your Soul chose for you eons ago.* And on the Earth plane, making that choice is very important and also a great blessing.

Asking this question about the Holocaust feels like leaving all safety behind. But okay, I am ready.

If one were to look at all of humanity as part of the being that is called Earth, and if you look at humanity as a whole, as **one** being within the family of beings of the Earth, then you might say that this Human Being is unconsciously needing to "hit bottom" like an alcoholic might unconsciously let his life totally fall apart in order to get on the road to recovery. In a much more complex way and on a level that has cosmic importance and impact, the being called Humanity is at that place. The atomic bomb and proliferation of nuclear weapons are, like the Holocaust and other mass murders, aspects of this same impulse to "hit bottom" playing out on Earth, but the human race as a whole does not yet have this awareness. As long as the drinker wants to go on drinking, he lets himself believe that greater consumption will make him feel better. At some point, however, when things get bad enough, he hits bottom and realizes that the addiction only held the illusion of help or relief or satisfaction. It only masked his pain and enabled him to avoid his problems temporarily.

Just so, **the human race holds tightly to the ILLUSION that nuclear weapons and all the other deadly technologies it has created, will somehow make it safer, ensure survival. You believe in war in general. You are addicted to wealth, power, ideological fanaticism, religious and sexual discrimination and control. You believe you have the right to wage war in the name of all of these addictions, just as the individual addict justifies stealing and even killing to get his fix. And just like the individual addict is unable or does not want to read the signs that he is killing himself with his continued use, you as a race continue to indulge in and** *justify your addictions without regard to the terrible impact on all of human development and future human functioning as well as on all other life forms. The "high" of power, wealth and one-upmanship is so intoxicating that the long-term effects do not register, or even if they do, they are ignored. You are NOT making yourselves safer; you are sealing your own fate.*

*Continued addiction demands an intensification of **denial**. You see the truth of this in the behavior of the individual addict. Can you not see it is true for the entire race? We believe you ARE beginning to break through denial and acknowledge some of the effects of your addictions, but you are not quite ready to give them up.*

*Another way of saying this is that ego loves its illusions of power. It loves its imagined sense of control. It loves right and wrong, good and bad, have and have not. It is invested in winning the game, coming out on top. **It keeps raising the stakes like the gambler who doesn't get it and doesn't seem to care that he is gambling his home away.***

The intervention needed for the human race is Soul intervention.** It is consciousness of and alignment with the true purpose of human existence, which can only come from Soul consciousness, not ego. The race of humans stands on this brink, hitting bottom so to speak, and hitting it again and again to Push this Awareness Through, **to YOU. Not to somebody else, but to YOU, ALL OF YOU.

For the individual addict who wants to manipulate, deceive and blame others, and who WANTS TO KEEP ON USING, you know that his only hope of recovery lies is taking responsibility for HIMSELF and discontinuing his use. In the very same way, you as a race cannot continue forever to avoid the consequences of your addictions with self-deception, blame of others and continued use of your intoxicants. Recovery will require a collective sense of responsibility.

Healthy family members intervene with the addict they love, and confront him with his impact on himself and on them, even at the risk of anger and rejection and even violent response. Just so, certain Souls offer themselves up to confront the human race with the severity of the impact of its increasing addiction to domination, to belief in good and evil, and to suppression of "other." These are the martyrs of the race — those who give their lives so that you all may see and transform your ego consciousness a little sooner.

God and Soul hear that call, even if you as a race do not yet sufficiently hear it. In exactly the same way that God and Soul hear you and are intervening with you personally, God and Soul, who love you ALL dearly, are intervening globally.

*So, difficult as it is to hear, and We **know** it is difficult to hear, it is the big things, where hundreds and thousands and millions of people die in an instant, that take a special place in what is now unfolding. You heard Us say that a mass amount of energy is released at those times and you wanted to shut down. It is true. Whenever spirit or Soul leaves body, energy of course is released. What you also heard Us say is that in these particular experiences like the Holocaust and Hiroshima, in ALL exterminations large and small, the energy of each Soul leaving the Earth, and all those Souls combined, sends up a cry to God that reverberates through the universe. And the force of this combined energy draws corresponding energy, through magnetism, down from Above. This is Our best translation for something that is not entirely translatable. You asked, in the Holocaust lifetime, to be a part of this voice that is being sent out, this call for help for the human race. Many asked, many Souls like you. It was a "sought" experience and an honor to be given a body for that purpose.*

I could barely hear this. Pictures from concentration camps stabbed at my heart. I tried to push them out of my mind but could not. At the same time, Their words held the promise of cool balm on scorched flesh. Could I embrace the idea that there was a higher purpose, even for this most hideous nightmare of human behavior? But then I had to ask myself, why, actually, would it be any less likely that a large group of Souls would martyr themselves for the sake of us all, than that one brave individual would? Could I begin to understand the suffering of Black people, Native Americans, gays, women, minorities of all kinds—could I begin to understand their suffering as Service to us all? Could I see them as heroic Souls who took on some of the most difficult parts in this human Play to call us all Home? Would I have the courage to be the voice of their sacrifice now, in this life?

It makes sense that what is true for the individual is true for the collective, that the microcosm and the macrocosm are the same. I just never thought of it that way. The messages of the most notable individual martyrs of the race, who we look to for courage and inspiration, are no different from the messages (could we but hear them) of the nameless, faceless victims of war, drugs, prostitution, poverty, or discrimination. So many children of God being crucified every day—the message of each and every one of them no different from the message of our most famous martyr—Jesus—could we but hear it.

This is not an easy thing to write. All these Souls incarnated into pain and suffering to call us Home? My mind grasps the idea; my heart still struggles to embrace it. Fear that this interpretation of horrific events could be misinterpreted as callous dismissal of the extreme suffering human beings have inflicted on one another, the suffering so many have endured and *still endure* – is terribly disturbing.

You fear that what We say could be misused as a rationale for serious evil in the world. And you fear somewhere down the road someone might say that the Path of Supreme Surrender is the Only Way and turn it into yet another dogma or that what We are saying could be twisted to mean that if Good and Evil are *only a story you were told and believed, then nothing is really Evil and people will feel free to do whatever they want. Let Us say this — **everything that can be used on the Horizontal Plane can also be misused.** Look at what happened to the wisdom and love of Jesus! It is the Law of Gravity that perpetuates the great Dualities inherent in the ego state, and therefore, as long as the human race lives in ego consciousness, it will continue to create Good and Evil out of just about everything. It is not your responsibility how any of this may ever be used. We are not saying you shouldn't care how it is used, but your responsibility is to listen to the call of Soul within yourself and follow where it takes you. Look at what has become of Christ's teachings. You certainly would not blame him for that!*

However, We know that you care about the quality and the source of this information and your hope is that it could be received with the same awe that you have experienced. But the issue for you is — do you dare to stand on what you have received? Do you dare to put it out with your name attached to it? Do you dare to say you believe it yourself? Before you worry about how all this could be interpreted and used, you have to be able to walk through the Fires of your own Path and actually share this.

You rebel against the idea that many, many Souls have chosen some of the most excruciating parts in the Play. But why? You are learning to understand and accept that you chose your individual part for a reason, that you chose just these energies to transform through the vehicle of your personal experiences. You are beginning to understand how Duality works. And that understanding has given you a great sense of meaning, purpose and direction in what otherwise has felt like a senseless and cruel Wilderness.

That understanding is giving you your life back. Can you begin to imagine how life-giving this understanding could be for others? So why is it so difficult to embrace that what is true for you is true for everyone? What is the difference between what happened to you and what has happened and is happening now to millions?

Nothing really. Except that that was me. Maybe I can accept it for me but not for other people, not for children.

You were a child.

I know, but as I said, that was me. I can accept that I guess.

We are all one body, parts of one body, if that helps. You are everything and you are at the same time an indistinguishable speck. We are all one Soul evolving, moving through experience to Being, moving through Time to Infinity, moving through separation to Oneness. You are not separate from them; they are not separate from you.

Your cry for help is humanity's cry for help. Your cry for help is Earth's cry for help.

***

I was stunned. Stunned by the dramatic shift in perception out of a previously unquestioned belief that Right is supposed to do battle with and overcome Wrong. Not that They are saying cruelty and murder are right or okay. They are *not* saying that. What They are saying, which was entirely new for me back in 1995, is that this battle will never be won! That ego consciousness is the *cause* of that endless battle! I was stunned by the brilliance of the parallel between the Path of an individual and the Path of the race, by the exact correlation between the microcosm and the macrocosm of human existence, that what we do as individuals is exactly what we do as groups and as a whole race of beings. Some perpetrate from a place of ignorance or pain or lust or greed (all dense and lawful ego energies) and others offer themselves up to testify to the power of the impulse to

Redeem love from Darkness—sometimes with their lives. Some of our greatest heroes are martyrs—Jesus, Gandhi, Martin Luther King. They gave their lives to Redeem Love. What I was beginning to understand was that on a Soul level, they knew what they were doing before they ever took body. They asked and agreed to play those parts for the sake of us all—NOT for the sake of making the "bad" people "good," not for the sake of proving them wrong or exacting retribution or converting them, but to wake us *all* up, to help us *all* get on the Road of Return, Return to Divine Love—**where we are all equals, equally worthy and equally loved in the eyes of God and Soul.** What I was beginning to understand was that the black people taken as slaves and the Native Americans who were slaughtered and the solo child killed at the hands of an abusive parent and the rape victim who is blamed for wearing that short skirt—*all* are the martyrs of the race and all are calling us to wake up to the Road of Return.

I was stunned, too, by the magnitude of the call for help we are emitting as a race without perhaps knowing it, in the same way that psychologically we are just now beginning to understand that an individual's acting out and dysfunction are a call for help for the family. Stunned by the idea that *ours* is a call for help for the Family of Mankind, and that God and Soul hear that call and are responding. And stunned, too, by the magnificent Revelation of a Soul purpose behind all of it, particularly the human suffering that has always seemed to me utterly heartbreaking and beyond imagination or understanding.

As a race, we seem to keep judging human dynamics as right and wrong in an effort to believe we could have control. Perhaps the question of why there is so much apparent pain, suffering, injustice, killing and death in the world, is the one of the great questions behind the formation of all religion—why there is Evil and how to become Good. Perhaps it is only normal, in our ego consciousness, to project our feelings and fears inward onto ourselves and outward onto others and assume this "Evil" is someone's "fault" or our own fault. And if there is fault, there is blame, and if there is blame, there is judgment and consequence, and then *there is more suffering.* All the while, various religions offer a multitude of formulas of belief and action that are supposed to save us from the human condition, make us "good" and "righteous" in God's eyes. And then we go around trying to force that formula down everyone's throat, including our own — until the next great answer appears.

The Duality of Domination and Submission takes over and we try to force ourselves and others to please a God who we believe holds our lives and our Souls in His Hands of Judgment. And so the cycle of suffering continues.

Even so, I don't know that I will ever fully understand why it was set up this way for human beings on this Earth. I'm not sure that understanding is fully possible while in ego consciousness. But it seems that it WAS set up this way — that we asked and were asked to make this journey from separation to reunion, from Darkness to Light, from the war of Duality to the Oneness of Divine Love. They are showing us how to leave the world of judgment behind, how to breathe this and all the vibrations and energies of all life forms through ourselves, through the Cross inside, and transform it all, one issue, one experience, one relationship at a time.

They are asking us to step out of our bondage to the right and wrong of What Is, to see Teacher in everything, to see what there is for us to *learn* from What Is rather than judge it. This is so difficult even with a single personal relationship, let alone global human relations, and yet it seems the same principle applies. What exactly did my Soul come here to *learn* from ALL that is playing out on the entire Earth? This is the question that is addressed in so much of the wisdom that came to me from Them. And it is a question that couldn't be more relevant today. How do we get out of the war between Good and Evil that has the potential to kill us all?

As I write these words, I am overwhelmed by a question of my own. It is so easy and automatic to ask why God would allow such suffering. But what if the question for us right now is **WHY DO WE ALLOW IT,** even from the standpoint of what we know, in our ego consciousness, about the consequences? And if we say we don't allow it, we pass laws, we create good ideologies, we put bad people in jail, we fight wars to stamp out evil- well, maybe it is time to look and see if what we are doing in the name of Good *is really working*. Does a belief in Good and Evil ultimately serve us? Where has it gotten us? We ask this question as a matter of course in so many areas of human life. Is this the most efficient engine? What is the healthiest diet? How do we cure this disease with the least adverse side effects? We ask constantly if what we are doing is working *except in certain areas*. And those are the areas where we hold the deepest unquestioned beliefs and where we then behave as if it is *heresy* to question those beliefs.

When a child in school hits other children, won't do his homework, is addicted to TV or drugs, steals, bullies, or destroys property, we don't hesitate to consider his behavior unacceptable and self-destructive. More recently, in the field of psychology, we understand these behaviors to be a cry for help. The acting-out child is now understood to be the symptom bearer of a dysfunctional family. He calls to the pain in the family like a fever calls to an infection in the body. What if we could begin to see the biggest symptom bearers of the human race — terrorists, tyrants, rapists on all levels — what if we could see them as symptom bearers for the dysfunctional and collapsing Family of Man? What if we could see the most outrageously destructive human behaviors **as humanity's cry for help for the Family of Man.** And who is listening? We wonder why God isn't listening, but what is our own response? And unfortunately, it seems we often blame those who cry the loudest and the longest. As a race, we blame our own victims exactly the same way abusive or neglectful families blame acting-out children as bad seeds, as deserving of abuse, and thereby justify mistreating them.

This is what I know as a psychotherapist: the behavior of the individual cannot be understood apart from an understanding of the family system dynamics he lives in. The most acting-out children are acting out something that *isn't working* in the family and the immediate culture. How can it be otherwise then that the most destructive individuals and groups worldwide *are not also acting out something that is not working in the Family of Man*?

Even so, I have no answer to human suffering that fully satisfies my own ego consciousness. I am still heartbroken by the escalation of our cruelty to one another. On that level I just wish we could love each other and make all the pain and hardship go away. But I do understand that for the most part that we *live* in ego consciousness, and as long as we live in ego consciousness we are subject to the laws that govern it. As long as we live in ego consciousness we will keep playing out the drama of the great Masculine/Feminine divide and the resulting intensification of Domination and Submission, Good and Evil, Love and Hate, Have and Have Not, and therefore we will continue to suffer as we now do. It seems the only possible Light in this Darkness is to find the *Light* of our own Souls and share that with one another, to find the *Love* of our Souls and give it away for free.

Chapter 13

An Evolutionary Leap

$\mathcal{A}$ s They took me higher and higher above the Play of human consciousness and the densest levels of the Horizontal Plane, where it had been nearly impossible to see beyond the thick black smoke of destruction, I was shown another amazing panoramic view of the landscape we inhabit and the challenges the human race is facing globally.

There is a void that is being felt on Earth. Through the course of evolution from your ape-like ancestors, you humans have developed enormous capacities. To put it very simply — there was intense focus over many ages on the development of the human body and psyche **as a "vehicle" for a certain kind of Soul expression.** *This was the* **INTENT** *behind the evolution of your species. There was an original agreement with God in which Soul began the process of a specific type of adaptation to the animal body creating the first human creatures. This Soul intent has* **informed and directed** *the development of the upright body, brain capabilities, language, tool-making, technological abilities, the development of complex abstract thinking and feeling processes, and the development of increasingly complex and interdependent social structures.*

This process began with the growth and development of the capacities of the individual vehicle and at each step along the way, were you to break it down, every advance made in response to this evolutionary impulse brings human beings into greater and greater contact with each other, greater interdependence, and increased need for cooperation. At the very same time, as animals, competition for territory and resources brings you into greater conflict. These apparently opposing forces of interdependency and competition create part of what We call Sand.

On the Horizontal Plane, Soul's original adaptation to body has manifested as "advances" in human functioning in countless ways — technological advances in food production, medicine, communication technology, social organization, weapons production — to name only a very few. These evolutionary "advances" allow you to compete more successfully for the perceived supply, while, at the same time, the interdependence needed to produce the supply grows exponentially. These very advances have brought you, as a race, to a lawful critical evolutionary juncture. **You are experiencing a massive escalation in the tension between the undeniable need to work together to survive, while at the very same time you are fiercely competing for the resources you need (or think you need). You are at a climax of experience in regard to the tension of these opposites. It will take an enormous evolutionary leap of consciousness to adapt to this new world climate and survive.**

A leap in consciousness as regards the relationship of the part to the whole is what is trying so hard to push through at the present time. The part cannot continue to imagine that it is separate from the whole or that it can now survive independent of the whole.

This is the Sand from which you are asked to make Pearls. The challenges you face today are not random. They are what you as a race came to take on. This is what you came into human form on Earth to do — to transform all the apparent conflicts and dilemmas you face in your ego nature into Pearls of Soul consciousness.

Every aspect of ego consciousness, every bit of Sand a human being takes on to transform within himself into consciousness of Soul and Oneness, will manifest in some knowable form on the Horizontal Plane according to that person's Soul Path — through his actions and vibrations. That manifestation is his Soul contribution to the

Return of all. Whether your Soul wants to express itself by championing minority rights or creating beautiful art or smiling at strangers or turning your life around in prison – every effort you make to leave a consciousness of Duality and the opposition inherent in Duality, every effort you make to move out of judgment and see the Teacher in experience, and listen to the Teacher for YOU, contributes to Pearl formation and the Return of all. We cannot say this loudly enough or often enough.

The focus on the survival of the individual – whether it is of the individual person, the individual nation, ethnic, religious or other group that perceives itself as separate from and in conflict or competition with any part of the Race of Man – is actually now what is ensuring your demise as a species. The focus on the survival of the individual provokes you to compete harder, dominate more forcefully, take more, build bigger weapons and kill more people. The evolutionary leap before you now is about consciousness of the Whole and the urgent need to function in your human life here on Earth, for as long as you have it, from Consciousness of the Whole, love of the Whole, and active attention to the highest good of the Whole.

This consciousness is not available through a purely ego-centered existence, though many, even in their ego nature, are more and more aware of the decreasing viability of the species if it stays on its present course. True consciousness of the Whole and the ability to create real Pearls from the intense Sand inside your shell comes from the growth and development of Soul consciousness. Why? Because only in Soul is Duality transcended. The extremes of Domination and Submission you play out in ego consciousness and which you fuel with the belief in Good and Evil, can only be healed in Soul consciousness. As long as Domination/Submission is the name of the game, there can be no viable consciousness of the Whole. There are a number of philosophies and ideologies that approach this understanding, but ego alone cannot embody the awareness that your mutual survival depends on.

The evolutionary leap facing the human race today is the evolution out of ego consciousness into Soul consciousness. Spearheading that leap is the reunion of the Masculine and Feminine, because the principle of Domination and Submission, which arises out of that Duality, perpetuates competition, perpetuates denial of your addictions and denial of your increasing interdependence, and perpetuates and reinforces your separation from yourselves, from each other, from your Mother Earth and from the Divine, which contribute to escalating violence and unending war.

The human race now faces massive changing external conditions that threaten its survival as never before. Why as never before? Because you yourselves have created most of conditions that threaten to wipe you out. Ego consciousness has created the conditions that threaten to wipe you out. Therefore, if ego consciousness IS the primary obstacle to your survival, then the evolutionary leap confronting you is the leap out of ego consciousness altogether!

This is why We have come.

Chapter 14

Adam and Eve; Pleasure and Pain

ore and more understanding of the Laws of Gravity flooded in on me — as well as the urgency to shift our consciousness now.

*The pain being experienced worldwide by so many human beings today, **the pain at human hands, is calling you all Home, calling you all to this most incredible of all evolutionary leaps you have ever confronted as a race.** The pain the human race is experiencing is exactly like your individual pain, Phyllis. It is calling you to evolve your consciousness. All the Fires within and all the Fires without are calling you to this. These are exactly the Fires you came into body to stand in and not be burned.*

If all the parts were homogeneous within the whole, there would be no friction and therefore no Evolution. Now there is nothing wrong with homogeneity; it simply is not the principle running the show on Earth. When you rub two pieces of matter together you create friction, which creates heat, which eventually creates fire, and fire releases energy that is then used to transform whatever it comes in contact with. Just so, the universe, as you know it, runs on that same principle. Motion creates heat, heat creates fire, fire releases energy for transformation. You think this law applies only to what you call "matter," to meat cooking on a fire or wood burning down to ash or gas running an engine.

*However, this is only a partial understanding of the Circle of Fire. **Everything** in your known universe operates on this principle,* *not just what you call physical matter. There is also emotional matter and psychic matter and intellectual matter as well. All of these are matter in Our vocabulary and all of them are energy at their core, energy that has condensed out into different recognizable shapes and forms. Fire, on all levels, brings matter back to its pure energy state.*

*The Fire of Surrender is the pyre on which ego consciousness burns. It releases the pure energy held in ego, and that energy is taken up by Soul to create Soul consciousness **within** the incarnate form.*

*Therefore, what you call a path of persecution is always a path of the return of matter to its original energy state. Now, you must realize that the word persecution does not exist in Our vocabulary. We use it because that word is ego's only way to understand or define this particular path along the Outbreath and Inbreath of God on the Horizontal Plane. Along the Outbreath and Inbreath of God, there are only the parts you simultaneously asked and agreed to play – **all for the sake of the evolution of Soul consciousness through form**, all for the sake ultimately, of Return. We do not expect you to understand this as yet.*

*We tell you that you have created pain – hear these words – **you have created pain as a signal**. It is part of your experience in body, part of your experience in form. It was necessary for the human body to have a highly refined nervous system to respond to all kinds of stimuli to keep the body alive. The reason why excessive cold feels uncomfortable, why it feels painful, is because the human body can only stay alive within a certain temperature range. If there were nothing within the body to signal that you are leaving the safe temperature zone, you would unthinkingly die of hypothermia.*

*Pain is not what you think. You have deified pain just as you have deified pleasure. **On the plane of ego or the Horizontal Plane, the psyche and the emotions and the intellect ALSO can only exist safely within certain "temperature ranges."** When the limits of a certain range are pushed, a sensation sets in to alert the organism that it is in a danger zone. The intent is that you then **leave** the danger zone. You as a race, in this accelerated state of ego* *consciousness, do not read the signals, or do not listen to them, just as We said the addict does not or does not want to read the danger signals of his addictive behavior.*

And the main reason why this is so is that you have found ways, over time, to derive pleasure from these danger signals or, to put it simply—you have learned to derive pleasure from pain.

This is a very dense condensation of what We call ego energies. This is also what We would call another terrific force of Gravity. The force of Gravity is all that which holds you in ego consciousness, just like physical gravity holds your body to the Earth. Every action, every image, every fantasy, every thought in which an individual derives pleasure from pain, **and especially from the pain of another,** *holds you all on the Horizontal Plane that much longer. We are not talking about the pain of a stretched muscle that comes from exercising or the exhaustion that comes with great mental or emotional effort. We are talking about the pleasure or satisfaction that one individual (or group) derives from inflicting pain on himself or others with the express purpose of personal gain of some kind – the belief that some "good" will happen – some personal tragedy will be avoided if you sacrifice others, or you will have more power or righteousness or wealth if a certain part of yourself or others is repressed, subjugated or destroyed, or that you will please God if you convert the heathens, or that you will have the ultimate orgasm from rape or sadomasochistic sex.*

You have come to the place where as a race you no longer know the difference between pleasure and pain in more areas of human life than you know. Television is a great tool in the hands of this force of Gravity because it enables millions of people at a time to "enjoy" destruction, degradation, sadism, humiliation and hatred **without the least worry of feeling any of the danger signals** *We have called to your attention. This dynamic is further complicated by the fact that you have come to believe that a certain amount of pain – and sometimes a huge amount of pain – is* **required** *in order to achieve pleasure. You see pain as a prerequisite to pleasure, as the* *price you have to pay,* **and especially the price OTHERS have to pay,** *for your pleasure, and this only enforces and reinforces the power of this Duality.*

Pleasure is not a sin as so many religions have tried to assert. And therefore, you do not have to atone for pleasure by inflicting pain on yourself or anyone else. Pleasure is not a sin. The Duality of Pleasure and Pain is all part of the **glue** *that keeps you on the Horizontal Plane.* **This is one of the ways Gravity works, keeping you in a state of scrambling around here and there to eradicate so-called evil in yourselves and others.**

These beliefs are all incorrect readings of the original Map of Creation, or more accurately, they are all ego's reading of the original Map of Creation. They are all part of the Sleep of Forgetting. **There is no Hell, there is no place symbolically or otherwise, where Souls roast over eternal fires to pay for wanton pleasures that were displeasing to an all-powerful, judgmental and angry God.** *Pleasure and pain, as you understand them, are two sides of the same coin, two sides of one of the greatest Dualities governing ego consciousness.*

Adam and Eve AGREED to leave Eden, HAD to leave Eden, because that was the Plan, not because of wrongdoing. The story of Adam and Eve is the story of how the seeds of ego consciousness were sown. *This myth represents the Sleep of Forgetting that marked the beginning of the human journey through ego consciousness. It is the seed from which the Horizontal Plane experience for humans grew. Adam and Eve are the symbolic representation of how Duality was implanted into human consciousness. True knowledge of the origins of Good and Evil was lost to human awareness* **because The Sleep of Forgetting was part of the Plan.** *The Serpent in the story is the symbol of the Serpent Power that set this trance in motion.*

Adam and Eve are the symbolic representation of the birth of ego consciousness in the animal that evolved into a human being. *What they took out of Eden (what they brought to* *the Horizontal Plane) was the* **belief** *in Good and Evil that the world struggles with so fiercely today. In this one story, the whole plot of the Karmic journey of the human race is laid out. Masculine and Feminine energies are in two separate bodies and two separate psyches (active Assertion becomes separated from generative Receptivity), the natural pleasure of man and woman coming together is linked to the judgment of Good and Evil, Pleasure becomes cause for Pain, man is set against woman, the human is separated from the Divine and God is believed to be the Judge who throws you out of Paradise for your sins.* **This story is the symbolic representation of the birth of Duality in human consciousness and therefore the birth of ego. This is the Wilderness you asked to traverse on your epic journey through Separation to Reunion. This story was implanted, lawfully, you might say, for mankind to debate all the way Home.**

What Adam and Eve took out of Eden was lawful: it was the Sand of your human evolution, the Sand out of which you came to make Pearls for the Creator.

Ego believes Good must triumph over innate Evil and that triumph of Good will please God who will then allow you back into Heaven. Soul embodies the living truth that God is calling you Home **through the transcendence of Duality altogether, through embodying Divine Love in your own human Being in the face of all the Dualities ego will tempt you with along the way.**

Do you understand? **Pain signals that you are out of the safe zone for human existence. It exists to call you Home.** *The great circles you run around in, chasing pleasure and avoiding pain, or chasing pain to increase pleasure, and judging every aspect of that chase as either Good or Evil — those circles you run around in are a lawful part of the gravitational field that holds human beings to the Horizontal Plane.* **They are an original condition of human incarnation; they do not signify original sin.** *The Laws of Gravity provide the great Sand We speak of that you* *came here to transform into Divine Love. You were not born evil. No. A thousand times no. You were born into ego consciousness, which was lawful.*

*The belief in original sin was intentionally tied to the Masculine/Feminine, Male/Female split and it is what you came to Undo and Redeem for the Creator. You will understand this more as We go. For now, **let Us say that human pain is calling Humanity Home, just as your personal pain was what called you, Phyllis, to Us.** We wish there was another word for pain on Our side of the spectrum, but you see there is no real translation because it does not exist here where We live.*

Again, the story of Adam and Eve. Your version is that the two of them did something wrong and were cast out of Eden as punishment. Your version is that they defied God's orders and suffered as a result. But look at that belief—if mankind can defy God's wishes, then man is more powerful than God. Then God is not God. God is then more or less an angry parent who has lost control of his children. Kind of silly, don't you think? Or you believe that God so-called gave you "free will" — but then you aren't really free to use it? If you don't use it correctly, you are damned? A parent gives his child a blowtorch and says, "Don't touch that! Your fault if you get burned!" ???

*Our version is very different. Our version is that Adam and Eve, symbolizing the origins of the human race (not two actual people), knew exactly what they were participating in and that they consciously took on the myth of Good and Evil because that is what the human race was asked to do. They **left** Eden, so to speak, as an act of participation. Do you think God went to all the trouble of creating the world and the magnificent multitude of creatures and plants and physical formations only to have human beings ruin that Eden through stupidity and avarice and moral degeneracy?*

Adam and Eve are the symbolic representation of how the Law of Gravity took hold in the human psyche. *Human* *beings do not fall prey to the impulses of Good and Evil due to human failing. No one can do anything that is not allowed, that is not directed from Soul. This is the truth.* **Adam and Eve did not defy God—HUMAN BEINGS TOOK ON AN EPIC EVOLUTIONARY JOURNEY.**

Now We know you want to ask, then **everything** *that happens in the world is allowed by God? Yes. How could it be otherwise? God is either God or not God. God is Omniscient, Omnipresent, and Omnipotent or God is not. God is either Divine Love or God is not. There cannot be a middle ground. The Creator is either the Creator of ALL — all matter, all form, all intention, all states of being, all actions, all reactions — or God is not. It can only be one or the other. God, Oneness, is not a larger than life human being with human emotions and motivations and limitations.*

Then you want to say, so then God allows wars and abuse and rape and starvation and prejudice? Yes, in a sense you could say it that way. But you have to be very careful with that line of reasoning, because in and of itself it will bring you to false conclusions. Before you reach any conclusions about what God allows or does not allow, you must realize that you do not yet understand what you are seeing when you see these things you mention. We are trying to help you see it all in a different light, the light of Reality. Right now, you can only see it from the point of view of your ego mind, which considers all things as either good or bad. You are learning and We are helping you see, that the very same things look entirely different from the point of view of Soul. It is very important that you do not jump to any conclusions at this point. Hold an open mind.

When you asked to incarnate to participate in the Holocaust, you asked to be one voice among millions, all calling Us en masse to the aid of the planet in just the very same sense that you, Phyllis, have called Us to yourself in this lifetime. **Think about it—out of your personal pain, you called in a force of Soul to yourself. Out of the pain of millions, billions, does it not also make perfect sense that a commensurate force of Soul**

could and would be available to respond, and would be
desirous of responding? Are We not proof that there IS a
response coming?

Your life in Germany was a blessing lifetime if you can understand
that. It prepared you for this lifetime. You do not yet know what
the fires of Auschwitz created and released on an energy level. But
know this: **no one there died in vain.**

***

Today I find this concept both challenging and riveting — **pain**
is the signal that we are leaving the safe zone of our
existence. We do not hesitate to read pain in the physical
body as a clear sign that help is needed immediately. But in
our emotional, intellectual, and spiritual worlds, the signals
seem to be increasingly lost in the thick black smoke of
judgment, greed, addiction to our intoxicants, an un-
quenchable thirst for power, and all the **projections** onto self
and "other" that feed these dense ego energies. I've said
it before but feel compelled to say it again. In the world
of psychology, we know now that a hurting, destructive, or
self-destructive child **is calling for help for pain in the family**.

How are we not reading these same signals on a global
level — terrorism, genocide, oppression, extremes of poverty,
and destruction of our environment? How are we not
reading our worldwide human pain and the extreme
destructive and self-destructive attitudes and actions that
fuel it as a deafening and unceasing **CALL FOR HELP** for
the entire human family? Deafening might be the word — can
we not hear it? Deafening — so loud we cannot or do not
want to hear it for the sake of some perceived pleasure or
gain from projecting all that pain onto others and holding
fiercely to the belief that we can resolve it through blame
and domination and getting "more" of whatever we think
we need.

We do not condone such behavior in an individual family. We teach our children not to bully, steal, discriminate, or kill. We feel and grieve the pain of an individual drug overdose or suicide or homicide and in the best-case scenarios we move away from blame and look for causes. And we look for HELP.

What has happened to our human family?

There is undeniable mounting evidence that as a race of beings, we have left the safe zone of our own existence. **WE HAVE TO FEEL THAT PAIN if we are to move back into a safe zone**—and pray it is not too late to do that. Projection is the main way we do not feel that pain. This was the message to me personally all those years ago—**I had to feel my own pain deeply in order to transform it**. My pain, **our pain**, is the signal that Love is needed.

Sometimes I am at a loss for words…

Chapter 15

The Play

*D*espite the fact that I was still a mass of unformed cells inside an indistinguishable cocoon, gestating perhaps, but not at all ready to emerge into the light of even the most ordinary day, They spoke to me anyway, loved me unconditionally anyway, and Their Divine Light shone on me day after day. They met me wherever I was, in the smallest, most contracted, unlit places in my psyche, without the slightest judgment. And that is the nature of Divine Love.

I went to a meeting at Daniel's school and I always have the same experience. I see how much I want to share and participate but how fearful I am of saying the wrong thing. I am intensely aware of my desire to hide—my thoughts and feelings and even my body. After all these years and all this work, I am still afraid of being noticed by men, frightened of being judged and rejected, all the while still hoping some Prince Charming will notice me anyway, tucked inside my unformed wings. Over and over again I see that I am no one special, that I am so limited when it comes to interacting with other people. It is so hard not to lapse into self-criticism. I still try to breathe it all through.

It is humbling to realize that you are no one special on the Earth plane. And at the same time, you are Divine. But you see, so is everyone. Please hear this. You do not have to be special to receive what We have to offer. No one has to be special or different or exalted in any way. No one is or can be special anyway. There is no such thing in God's eyes. You are not favored because you receive this. You receive this because you asked for this experience, because it is a part of your path. Do you understand? Everyone gets to be, needs to be, and has to be exactly who they are, no more, no less. Moving out into the world a little bit as you did these past few days can help you see that the personality Phyllis is just another personality, one of millions.

Do not be dismayed by what you see and do not be overjoyed at what you see. Do not be tired at the thought of how far you think you have to go. Be exactly who you are, and stand in grace in that. Know that whenever you feel critical of yourself, that you are glued to a projection of ego that is glued to the law of opposites — good and bad, pretty and ugly, happy and sad. Find that place in the center, that place of steadiness IN SOUL. **Breathe the feelings through the Cross and see yourself moving up and off the Horizontal Plane, out of ego consciousness on the Inbreath, and then down and out across the Horizontal Plane as Soul energy manifesting, guided by God, on the Outbreath.** *This is the meditation of Surrender. You give your life energy to God and God shows you how to bring Divine Love back to yourself and your fellow travelers on the Horizontal Plane.*

We are never critical of you or anyone. We do not see through eyes that define in terms of the opposites found in the ego realm. When We say at times, We love you, it is not the same love you know in your incarnated state where one day you love someone and the next day you hate them. Love for Us is a state of Being, **a condition of Being,** *not a feeling that comes and goes dependent on actions and reactions and circumstances and needs and moods. There is no hate in Our realm, and there is no hate in God's realm, which are one and the same. Therefore, there can be no eternal Hell that God casts the so-called wayward Soul into.*

Know this — that at your place on the Path you can expect to go back and forth between the illusions of good and bad, right and wrong, connected and not connected, at a higher and higher pitch, intensity, velocity, and "temperature" as part of the process of moving out of that realm altogether. When you feel caught in any given Duality, bow to whatever the apparent obstacle is, hard as that may be, and **rather than saying, "What have I done wrong?" say, "Nothing is an accident. What is here for me to see, to learn, to Surrender?"**

I told a friend about the past lives I was seeing in therapy. Her response was, "Wait until you see the ones where you were the perpetrator!" Since most of the lives I saw were similar in theme to the witch life, I immediately felt abysmal shame. So, you think you've just been the little martyr victim, Phyllis? You think you were always the innocent who was so terribly wronged? Shame on you! You just wait until you see all the people *you* slaughtered!! It didn't take much to topple me over.

You were disturbed when your friend asked you about whether you had gotten to the lives where you were the perpetrator. You hadn't seen past lives like that except perhaps the one in which you saw yourself hanged. Her question shook your belief in yourself and again brought up a lot of self-judgment. Now you think you have to see lifetimes as some awful perpetrator. You feel it would be presumptuous of you not to think that you were the "bad guy" as well as the "good guy." And Our answer to you is this: What difference does it make? **We are telling you that bad and good are illusions—very powerful, but illusions. Therefore, bad guys and good guys are also illusions. They are PLAYERS on opposite sides of the stage.** *One isn't better than the other in Reality. We are not talking about ordinary life here. We are talking about the Road Home. And on the Road Home, We are telling you that the parts you played are only the* **parts you played.** *They are not WHO YOU ARE. Would it make you more believable, more humble, more self-effacingly acceptable if We showed you lives in which you hated or stole or murdered? And in whose eyes would you be more acceptable?* **Because if you believe you have to "confess" to sin, to "badness" and admit fault and** *somehow atone in order for God to love you—and We know in ego consciousness of course you believe you have to—you will have a hard time grasping that God's Love is for everyone, all the time, equally, NOW.*

We are not saying that it should be all the same to you if you help your neighbor or murder him, if your governments help the poor or enslave them, if you rescue endangered species or take the last tusk or the last hide and wipe one more creature off the face of the Earth. Of course, We are not saying that.

What We are saying is that loving the Soul in all things—seeing, honoring, encouraging and feeding Soul in all creatures and all beings—is the WAY OUT of the mess you are in. It is the only WAY OUT of the endless war between Good and Evil. What We are saying is that working with the energies that keep you stuck in the war between Good and Evil (and all Dualities) and transforming those energies in yourself into Divine Love to the very best of your ability, is the way to leave war altogether.

This is how you wake up from The Sleep of Forgetting.

Religion says, "Look for your sins and atone. Look for the sins in others and make them atone and become good." We say, "Look for God in you and shine the light of Soul everywhere you go. Look for God in others and do everything in your power to let their light shine. Look for God in everyone and everything and get off the Wheel of Karma, and together you light the way Home.

When you create plays in your human world, you usually have some version of a hero and a villain or you have some "light" force or impulse countered by a "dark" force or obstacle. You have a tension of opposites, a playing out of themes that build toward some dramatic climax. You don't say the actual people playing the bad guys are evil and the ones playing the good guys are actually heroes. When the play is over, they all go home to their ordinary selves and *their ordinary lives. You **know them as actors**, and when they leave the stage and go home, they are not the parts they were playing.*

In the very same way, God has created a Play and you are all players. You are all Soul wearing different costumes playing different parts, creating a tension of opposite forces, playing out world themes, building toward a dramatic climax. *It is only on the Horizontal Plane that the climax you are looking for is that of Good conquering Evil, the good guys beating some version of the bad guys in the end.*

*In the world of God, the climax, you might say, comes when **you STEP OUT of all your roles, take off the costumes of ego and personality altogether, ALL TOGETHER, and go HOME to your true nature, which is SOUL.***

This is so incredibly beautiful, so real. I have never heard anything like this. The heart/truth of it vibrates inside me. I want to be capable of shining the light of Soul just as You describe. And yet I still do not understand the "why" of all this. I don't think I can at my level of development, but it seems to me that there has to be much more of an explanation about the mass cruelty and suffering we experience here on Earth than I now can conceive of. I just fear that Your words could imply that it's all the same if you are the murderer or the one murdered.

In a theater, no one actually gets shot or killed. In our embodied life, the bullets kill, the blood is real, the children are left parentless. The players may go home to God, but they don't go home to their families. Are we not supposed to try to stop the pain and suffering, the injustice and cruelty? It feels like we are hovering on the brink of extinction and when I look at the world as it is, it is very hard to believe that the massive changes that appear to be needed could possibly happen in time to save us.

*We hear your thoughts and questions and We will say this: Of course, on the most basic level of your human existence you try to stop the murderer or the rapist or the thief, just like you do everything in your power to help your daughter stop using drugs. You may be successful or you may not. But you will go on trying. It is exactly the same in the world at large on the Horizontal Plane. Sometimes a murderer or a thief will be stopped and prevented from doing further harm or even reformed, and sometimes not. As individuals, communities or nations, some of you will go on trying to stop or prevent these destructive acts. Of course you will. This is basic survival. But what We are trying to tell you is that **there will be no resolution on this level**. This PLAY of Good and Evil is an inherent part of your ego existence. **The way out of this Play is to leave ego consciousness.** That is what We are trying to tell you. That is what We came here to help you learn how to do.*

God created oysters and Sand and the possibility of Pearls. This is the truth. Go out and create Pearls from all the Sand you have put inside each other's shells.

Help me understand my part, Surrender my part, and use all the energy still held in my part for Your purposes, God. Help me know the Soul Part You want me to play on the Road of Return and give me the strength to walk that road. Help me take this costume off, so that I can see who I really am.

Chapter 16

The Breath of the Cross

$\mathcal{A}$ nd then the "how to" of transforming ego energy into Soul energy, was shown to me in much greater detail. In a meditation, as I was visualizing breathing ego energy through the Cross, an amazingly beautiful image of what the meditation of Surrender actually looked like came to me. The image was so alive, I felt I had to paint it and so I did. (You can see that original image on the back cover of this book. I have included a black and white version here.)

The meditation is called the **Breath of the Cross Meditation** or the **Meditation of Supreme Surrender**. In my vision I saw a Fire in the First Chakra and that energy moved up through all the chakras and out of the body through the Crown Chakra at the top of the head. Then I saw the energy connect with God or Oneness, represented by a star. And finally, the energy circled down from God and entered the Heart Chakra, filling it with Divine Love. I could feel the intense vibration of Love in my own heart. This meditation outlines the transformation of ego energy into Soul energy. It symbolizes the process of "burning up" ego consciousness in the First Chakra, and the energy released from that burning then rises up and begins the process of transforming the ego energies held in all the chakras.

Just as Fire on the physical plane transforms matter and releases energy that can be harnessed and used, so Fire on a spiritual level releases the energy held in our ego consciousness and frees it to be taken up by Soul, so that Soul can express itself through us in our human form. This is the meaning of the Fire symbol at the base of the spine. In very simple terms, this meditation is about Surrendering ego experience to God and asking that it be transformed and used for the highest good and speediest Return of all beings. After intersecting with Oneness at the star, the energy comes back down into the Heart Chakra, the home of Teacher within each of us, which shows us the way God and Soul seek to manifest through us.

Whatever the experience or feeling in the moment is, They said to visualize it burning in the Fire at the base of the spine, see the pure energy it contains being released from the hold of ego and "breathe" that energy up through all the chakras, out the top of the head, give that energy to God and Soul (the star), and breathe Divine Love back into the Heart Chakra to infuse one's entire being. The energy moves upward on the Inbreath and back down into the heart on the Outbreath accompanied by one long Om sound on the Outbreath. They said to repeat this over and over again for as long as desired.

Later the **Breath of the Cross Meditation**, or **Meditation of Supreme Surrender**, was greatly expanded on, and I was given detailed information about the chakra energies and functions. But in the beginning, this is how the meditation was shown to me and this is the meditation I did. My understanding of the Cross also expanded. I saw the Cross of energy *inside* me, a Cross formed by the intersection of the Horizontal and Vertical Planes. I saw how energy is released from the hold of ego consciousness (the Horizontal Plane), given to God, and returned into my being at the Heart Chakra to be manifested through me on Earth with my fellow man. The intersection of God's Divine Love with my human heart forms the Cross within me and it represents Soul Consciousness awakening in my heart and in my being. It is the place where the Horizontal Plane experience becomes the food for my Vertical ascent and where the Road of Return begins.

I had no particular association with the chakras at the time I saw this vision. I knew what chakras were, more or less, but I had no knowledge of their energies nor had I ever worked with them. But it was clear that the chakras were very important in the Breath of the Cross Meditation. I was being shown that **what there is to do** with the pain of ego consciousness—the pain within myself—has everything do with clearing the chakras of ego and lighting them up with Divine Love. As this information unfolded, I would come to see yet again the direct relationship of the microcosm and the macrocosm, the individual and the global, and how we as individuals can use this same meditation to work with the painful chaos of ego wreaking havoc around the globe. Much of this material will be found in Book III.

The Fires of the Horizontal Plane could consume me or I could learn to use and transform the massive energies they held. I was being given an actual practice for how to begin that transformation process. A whole new chapter of the work with Them had just opened, and a whole new piece of the Map was unfolding. Like everything else, I could not have known then where it would take me.

Then They spoke about Jesus on the Cross.

The nails and the crown of thorns and the agony of the body of the Christ symbolize a transformative experience. It is very interesting to Us from Our point of view that the Crucifixion is seen as such an amazing event when in fact you crucify each other daily. Why is what happened to you or what happened to any of the people you work with, for instance, any less of an event? The difference is that Christ was recognized as the Son of God. And yet, **We are here to tell you that you are all the Sons and Daughters of God** *and the Crosses you carry and are "nailed" to are great transformative opportunities just as Jesus's was.* **Such experiences are sought by the Soul as food.** *The experience of Christ was also different from the experiences you are familiar with* **because he knew, even at the worst moments, that he was the Son of God and he knew exactly what was being transformed. The Crucifixion of Jesus is the symbolic representation of the transformation of humanity's ego pain into Soul Love, ego mortality into Soul Immortality. And that is really what he came here to demonstrate for you all, among many other things. He did not come to save you from sin. He came to tell you that you, too, can know yourself as the Son of God and that you, too, can transform the Cross you believe you are nailed to into the direct path of your ascension.**

Christ was the embodiment of Divine Love and Wisdom. That is what he manifested on the Horizontal Plane. When he said to "turn the other cheek," he was giving instruction on how to begin the process of "un-sticking" from the projected ego energies of others. He was not giving instruction to be a doormat or a voluntary victim or to take some imagined "high road." Christ was not a victim and he was not above it all. He was absolutely active in his apparent passivity. He took the sheer force of the fear, hatred and ignorance that nailed him to the Cross (the ego energies projected onto him by others) and he "Crossed" it with the power of Love/Wisdom running through his heart. He "ascended" with the force of an explosion on the power generated from Divine Love transforming massive ego energies.

This is exactly what you are being asked to do, you who hear this call. You are being asked to transform massive ego energies, not only your own but also those of your times, as Jesus did, participate as Jesus did, and ascend as Jesus did.

*If We could say it in terms you are becoming familiar with, Jesus ran all the energy coming toward him from his persecutors, which was ego energy on a Planetary level, up from the base of his spine and out the top of his head, brought it back down into his heart as pure "illuminated" energy, and along with all the illuminated energy he already embodied, he ascended, he Returned. He modeled the transformation of ego energy into Divine Illumination. He did not remove ego energy from others or die for their "sins." It was their **projected ego energy** that he transformed, not his, because, as a Master, he did not operate in ego. This is a key to a door you have not yet passed through.*

*Jesus did not live in the realm where the Laws of Gravity apply, and that is why some say his body went with him. When an incarnate being transcends the Laws of Gravity on all levels, he is no longer subject to them and therefore will manifest on the Earth plane in ways impossible for others to do, comprehend, or believe, even when they see it with their own eyes. That is why you hear stories that Christ walked on water. He was transforming energy all his life, everywhere he went, but the external manifestation was only a symbol for the real message, which was to transform the energies within. Raising someone from the dead, bringing them back to life, is a symbol of the Life in Soul **you** came to raise from all that is not "living" in your psyche and in your heart. This is what Jesus came to teach you to do. This is what the Cross symbolizes, and this is where the Path of Supreme Surrender will take you. The Breath of the Cross Meditation is your road to this end.*

I began to visualize and breathe Fire up from the base of my spine through all my chakras in the pattern They showed me. Right away I felt energy most noticeably in my heart and throat. Even now as I say this today I can feel the energy intensify in those two chakras. The meditation clearly "works on" the places where ego has the tightest grip *and* Soul has the greatest gifts to offer.

Chapter 17

The Morning Prayer

*T*his is the prayer We give you to help you orient yourself toward what We have called the Vertical Plane and the Path of Surrender that takes you there. We call it The Morning Prayer.

I bow to myself
I bow to the Guru within
And the Guru without
Who are one and the same

I bow to all that is
All that was
And all that will be
With Supreme Surrender

I am not afraid
I step willingly
And with a pure heart
Out of the way

And I have faith in God
And in my own Soul
Who are one and the same.

Supreme Surrender is that state in which all ego energy is surrendered to Soul, in order that Soul consciousness increasingly informs the thoughts, feelings, intentions and actions of the vehicle – you – and the totality of capacities housed in the human body. On the Horizontal Plane, this totality of capacities is driven by ego consciousness.

*When you are in the throes of your deepest and most unconscious ego projections, Surrender means remaining open to seeing and feeling those projections and taking the power out of them, taking your energy as much as possible **off the Horizontal Plane and back into yourself**, no matter how difficult it is to do that – and it is always difficult – and giving it all to God, to be used **through you, through Soul in you, for the highest good of all. It means learning from experience what Soul has to teach you and leaving the realm of judgment.***

I wish with all my heart and Soul to be with You. I don't even know what to ask sometimes anymore, the picture becomes so big and yet I in form am not big. I am in awe. I know I am standing on holy ground, and whatever You wish is what I will try with all my heart and Soul to hear and to do and to follow for the rest of my life here on Earth. I am so grateful that I don't even know what to do with myself except meditate and write and breathe with You and remember to do it. I know that all my prayers are heard, that I am no longer lost. I am found. I know now that we are all going Home, however long it takes, whatever comes across our Paths.

*You would like Us to say more to you about "stepping out of the way." The words of the prayer are somewhat of a redundancy. When you release your fear to Faith in God and your own Soul, you **are** stepping out of the way. We have added the words, "willingly and with a pure heart," especially to emphasize that (from the vantage point of ego consciousness) this is a process that you **choose** to participate in. Another way to say it is that you allow all the protective mechanisms organized by your ego over eons to be laid at God's feet and you walk only in God's protection and at God's* *direction after that. This means you allow Soul to govern the body, the mind and the heart. There is nothing to do at the moment to facilitate this happening other than to continue your work of Undoing, your work of Surrender, breathing, meditating and writing.*

"I bow to all that is, all that was and all that will be," means I accept everything within and everything without, I receive it rather than reject it. I do not resist it. I take it in and digest it all until I have eaten my whole self up. Then I am done with this life as I know it and I enter another realm of life. It is the same principle for the race and for the planet and for God. This is the Ouroboros, the Serpent eating himself. This is the universal or cosmic mechanism of Self-generation as far as you can understand it.

***

And then, after this initial explanation of Supreme Surrender was complete, I saw Swami Muktananda for the last time in a meditation.

He told me not to see him anymore as he appears in his picture. He said it is okay to have the picture and look at it, but to remember that he no longer inhabits that form. He said he is not really a man anymore and to see him as energy rather than a face or a body in orange robes. He said, *I am the Fire burning in you now and burning all around you. I am also the Serpent. I am everywhere – inside you everywhere and outside you everywhere. I am Fire now because you are working with Fire. When you are no longer working with Fire, I will be cool Water. I appear as Swami Muktananda in my approach to you but I am no longer Swami Muktananda.*

This is the Way of Supreme Surrender. Supreme Surrender is Surrender to What Is. Before you can truly understand What Is, you must Surrender completely to What Is. Before you can see through God's eyes, you have to breathe God inside you.

At the moments of my most Divine connection, at the moments when Love was poured into my heart and Light was poured into my mind from so many directions, at those moments there was no judgment and no comparison at all. There was only Being, and Being seemed to be the equivalent of a vibration of Divine Love for which there are no adequate human words.

The key to that for me is expressed in the Morning Prayer. It is the prayer of Supreme Surrender, Surrender to What Is, All That Is. The direction is to bow to *everything* — accept, digest and transform everything I encounter —*everything*—inside and outside, to see everything as my greatest Teacher, as exactly that which Soul came into human form to experience and transform.

In a way, it is the simplest formulation in the world, but perhaps the most difficult of all to accomplish, because getting beyond judgment might be the hardest thing of all to do.

Chapter 18

Standing on Your Cross

*L*et Us explain more about standing on your Cross. This *has nothing to do with any image of you full of nails and it is not you bleeding to death as a martyr. Jesus was not a martyr. As We have said, he did not die for your sins. See yourself standing on the Cross **willingly,** consciously facing whatever you encounter, whether it appears negative or positive. Let's just say you feel rejected by someone. Allow that energy to pass through you as you **stay standing**. When the energy passes through the Cross, it passes through your heart. Within your heart is your Soul. Allow the pure, raw energy of your feelings, reactions and judgments to be given to Soul and God to be used for your highest good and for the highest good of all.*

This is how you "love your enemies." You don't have to like what people do and you don't have to "forgive" in the ordinary sense. You don't have to be silent or selfless and you don't have to "take the high road." Instead, you use everything that comes your way from others to fuel the power of Soul to manifest through you. In that way, it is impossible NOT to love others.

The Soul Seed, which lies in the center of the Cross, holds both the Map of your journey on the Horizontal Plane and also the blueprint of your ascension onto the Vertical Plane. So, you take all the energy of an event or feeling through the center of the Cross and you do that consciously and you do that willingly and you do that with your eyes open and you do that with an awareness of everything that you feel. You ask Us, you ask God, to use that energy in your ascending path rather than to take you further out on the Horizontal Plane. You do your best not to project hatred back onto that person, if it is a person. You don't project fear. You don't project anything back onto anyone. If there is energy that is ill intended, you pass it through this central place in you and out. Give all that energy to God to be used in whatever way God intends.

You can process any experience in this same way, positive or negative. Neither the positive nor the negative is who you really are. None of it is who you are. It is what you are experiencing. The Soul is the eye in the center of the storm—whether the storm is a beautiful windstorm on a sunny afternoon or a hurricane that is beating the landscape to a pulp. They are both manifestations of the Divine, but you are not either one.

We are not saying that you can't take joy in what is joyous. But know that joy and fulfillment are also the raw material you came into this body to use for your Soul's evolution through form. This is very different than just going out and spreading love and joy. And there is absolutely nothing wrong with going out and spreading love and joy. But that is not exactly what you are asking entrance into right now. Do not fear life experience and do not count on it. Count on nothing but your relationship with Teacher, with Us, with God and with your commitment to stay on this path. You know this to be the truth.

*You are learning to bend your emotional body. The emotional body is subject to the Laws of Gravity. Feelings fluctuate with the swing of all the Dualities—Masculine/Feminine, Good/Evil, Right/Wrong, Have/Have Not, Destruction/Creation, Pleasure/Pain. The emotional body is **glued**, so to speak, to the impulse to move from the perceived negative to the perceived positive, which is also a Duality. This is actually how Duality works as a mechanism of ego consciousness. The ego always strives toward whatever it perceives is the more desirable half of any given Duality. If something appears worse, you strive for what you believe is better. If you perceive negative, you want the positive, a perception of less* *creates the desire for more, and so on. Unending comparison and judgment are generated in this way and keep you in the tight grip of ego consciousness.*

Within your emotional center, there is the unconscious expectation (and sometimes conscious) that as you move closer to God and to Oneness, you will feel better. There is the expectation that all negative emotions will dissolve into positive ones. Underlying this assumption there is also the belief that if you feel what you would consider a negative emotion, then you are farther from God than if you feel what you consider a positive one. And there is automatically judgment that comes up about this.

*This assumption is part of the Duality of Better and Worse. What We are saying is that **any feeling** you have can be used as a stepladder to God if you are willing to climb up it, if you are willing to use the energy generated by any feeling for your ascent in a Vertical direction. This means you remove the energy from the Horizontal Plane **by removing judgment of it**, whether it is anger, fear, sadness, depression, anxiety, etc., and you Surrender it to God actively in the sense of breathing it around the Cross. This is the way given to you on your Path. This is not a passive under-taking. You do not just stand by and say, "I give this to God." God doesn't do it for you. You do it in relation to God. You do it with God, for the love of God in your heart and for the love of God in your Soul.*

Which is to say, do not judge any part of this process in terms of what you think you have and do not have as a feeling, an attitude, a mindset, a preoccupation or a fear. Have and Have Not are a Duality that belong to the ego plane. Therefore, when you find yourself worrying because you do not feel emotionally vibrant or even connected, when you worry that you do not have the right feeling for one on the Path, bow to that, and Surrender that as well. Surrender the power of all that you have held as either good or bad to God, move your energy off the Horizontal Plane with the help of the Cross, and experience Soul as distinct from ego in that very moment. This is the crucial first step in bending the emotional body off the

Horizontal Plane and up into the arc that curves away from the surface of the Earth, leaving the Laws of Gravity in its wake and moving toward intersection with the Great Circle of Being. This is part of what is depicted in the image of the Breath of the Cross Meditation you received.

This was so different from anything I had ever heard or believed. I judged myself harshly for feeling disconnected, lethargic, irritated, anxious, or in pain, for wanting to distract myself or avoid difficulty. In all the spiritual paths I had attempted to follow earlier in my life, I looked to others as role models of how I should "be." I tried to look centered, not complain, say what I thought was acceptable or what I associated with someone on a spiritual path. Yet all the while I agonized about how truly unacceptable I felt, all the ways I was not good enough and not doing enough to please the God I hoped to find. Never had I heard any concept of *using* — digesting, eating — all that I am, exactly as I am, as a spiritual practice. And I have to say that today, more than twenty years since They first came to me, I still fall easily into judgment of my emotional state, and that judgment continues to be food for my journey.

This step requires Faith, just as all previous and future steps require Faith. Every time you leave some aspect of the known world behind and allow yourself to move into the unknown that calls you from Soul, Faith is required. Not blind Faith, not Faith in an all-powerful external authority, but Faith in the guidance and messages received from your own Soul, however those messages may come to you, whether from a flower or Us or a client or your child or a charged collision of events or a moment of insight.

Uncomfortable, painful emotions are the most difficult, but keep passing them through, for as long as it takes, as difficult as it feels, as hot as the burning is, as much as you feel pulled into a dark space-just draw them consciously through your heart. Stand on your Cross and pray that this energy be used for your highest good, *for your speediest Return, for your deepest connection to God, to Soul, to your Teacher. Do this consciously, willingly, and with great presence and great love for your Master, who, as he has told you, may be seen as the Guru, may be seen as Swami Muktananda, may be seen as Jesus, may be seen as every experience, every person, you encounter. Bow down to this and consciously pray for this transformative process to occur. In this way, you don't create more projection and Karma on the Horizontal Plane. Stand on your Cross as Jesus did. Transform the energies that are yours to transform as he did. **Everything you transform in yourself, through the vehicle that is you, you transform for the world. ACCEPT ABSOLUTELY WHAT IS. Surrender with Supreme Surrender to WHAT IS, to the Guru, Soul and God, who is everything and who is everywhere. And We would like to add — AND WHO LOVES YOU.***

As I read these words today, I cannot help but feel that the challenge to keeping breathing everything through has never been greater or more urgent, at least in my lifetime. The darkness and the burning I feel in what seems to be an escalation in divisiveness, violence and hatred worldwide, terrify my ego self and call me to my Soul as never before. I remind myself that I am not alone, that millions of others are also feeling the call of their Souls, the call to Love of the highest order. I try to imagine what Jesus actually experienced as he endured the darkness of his times and the Cross he chose to bear. I try to imagine who he was able to BE in the face of his persecutors, and I try to tell myself that if he could Redeem Love in the face of Crucifixion, we can do it, too.

And at the very same time, in my heart of hearts, I pray that we could all see the Christ in each other now, and that all the crucifying could be over.

Chapter 19

Dark Energy

$\mathcal{P}$erhaps it is not a coincidence that They spoke next about Dark energies.

***

The breathing I was doing at that time was truly sending Fire up through my chakras. As Soul worked its miracle of "raising me from the dead," deeply stuck energies that were keeping me from living were unearthed and tossed into the flames. As a result, I felt compelled to talk about my writing with others, but sharing even a little bit only increased my fear of exposure and condemnation. I asked again why I was still so frightened.

There are crystallizations of dark energies that are created by individuals and groups of individuals. These energies are attached to both the Souls from which they emanated and to the Souls whose energies were invaded or perpetrated upon. **When ego energy is projected onto another and absorbed by the other, a Karmic attachment is created between the two.** *These are the energies you take back and give back in the work of Undoing. The energies that silenced you in the past and that you absorbed are still attached to you in their raw energy form wanting to silence you now. These energies come from this lifetime but also from past lives.*

I thought of fairy tales with ogres or sorcerers who capture people and turn them into zombies or put them into a deep sleep. Then when the sorcerer is killed or the hero frees the captured Souls, they all come back to their normal alive state. I wondered if these fairy tales were based on a long-forgotten understanding of how we come under the influence of energies projected onto us by others, and how we cannot be truly alive until we are freed from them. They were telling me that projected ego energies don't necessarily all come from present life experiences and relationships. They can carry over from one lifetime to another.

When you have a negative entity attached to you, like you have from the witch lifetime, where people with very powerful dark energy affected you and had power over you AND their power was not dissipated before you died, then a piece of your energy is embedded in that entity or attached to it and it to you. As you free yourself from this powerfully projected and internalized negative energy, the ones from whom it came lose their power over you. You have reclaimed your energy for yourself. When a person so-called "sells his Soul to the Devil," he doesn't really sell his Soul. He makes a conscious contract to give his ego energy up for some gain on the Horizontal Plane. He gives up a piece of his life force to a dark entity and allows it to be used for dark purposes, which are what you consider to be destructive forces on the Horizontal Plane.

*But you have to understand that when We say "dark entity," We are referring to a very dense condensation of **ego** energy — so dense that it blocks out light. We are not implying evil or sin or Satan. We are not saying that the Soul itself is darkened or affected in any way. We are saying that dense ego energies overshadow the Light Soul carries.*

On this very dense level, people either agree to participate in relinquishing part of their life force for some assumed gain — power, control, money, sex— or they are traumatized into a state where the energy is taken from them either overtly against their will or more subtly by manipulation. When they reclaim their captured energy, the power of the "dark being" is deflated and that dark being will often then go out and look for someone else or others to consume.

*On the plane of ego, those who are taken from often turn around and become those taking. This is the extreme end of the Law of Eating. The fairy tales are based on this reality. However, on the Road of Return it is understood that the Teacher **within** is the one who sets the captive free — not a fairytale savior who rescues the "good guys."*

*In Soul consciousness you "eat," only by permission and only for the highest good of all concerned. **So you see, the challenge for the Race of Man — to Undo the power of what We are calling Darkness, is now both a personal challenge and a global challenge, because in so many ways you are taking each other's energy globally through manipulation and force every hour of every day.***

Back in the 90's, I was focused on the personal aspect of this challenge. It was an evolutionary leap in itself for me to grasp that there were actual negative energies affecting me from outside my own psyche and that I could begin to identify and work with them. It was an amazing relief to understand that the darkness in my life was not further evidence of my unworthiness, but that the Darkness was exactly what my Soul came to work with. Today I am astounded by the profound significance and global relevance of what it means to "eat without mutual consent," and to understand the dark energies that influence our *collective* human psyche and play out in international relations. I am inspired by the idea that working with those dark energies on a personal level is a blueprint for working with them globally. But for now, back to 1995.

T was very interested in the subject of dark energies. Perhaps because of his training as a Shaman, the existence of dark entities was a given for him, a known experience. For me it was a totally new concept and one I found very disturbing. It sounded like sorcery to me. I did not want to believe there were unseen dark forces — the seen ones were bad enough. I understood that the wounds of childhood for most people have very lasting negative effects. And I was open now to the idea that unresolved issues and relationships from past lives are not all that different in their emotional and even physical impact. But I never thought about negative energy actually having a disembodied presence *outside* me. I only considered the negative energies I found *inside* me. I only thought about feelings, or even maybe vibes coming from others. I never thought about negative *entities* having power to hurt me. But if "They" are a distinct energy that is Light, and certainly They are not in body, then it only makes sense that there could also be distinct energy formations that are Dark that are also not in body. And because there is no darkness in Their realm, the condensations of dark energy They were referring to had to exist only on the level of ego consciousness.

In a session, T asked me to see what these negative entities were that were still around me. Very clearly, I heard,

It is a host of Black Magicians. And all that means is this: they are the representation of the crystallized energy of those around you, who, over lifetimes, worshiped money, power, sex and any combination of those three, who worshiped those things in the sense of deifying them, taking "blood money" to increase their store, which means literally exploiting, persecuting, killing, sacrificing others. They believed that through human sacrifice of whatever kind, they could extract the energy of their victims and use it for themselves. In their ego minds they might have even convinced themselves they were doing God's work, but on a pure energy level they were manifesting a most dense form of the energies of Destruction completely separated from the power of anything Divine at all. This is not mumbo jumbo; it is not sorcerers' talk from a fairy tale. It is how life in ego actually works and has accelerated and become denser, though often disguised under words like capitalism, communism, righteousness, or survival of the fittest. You see.

T asked me to get in touch with the part of me that was still connected to these Black Magicians.

I saw that it was the part of me that is still afraid of them and that I stay attached through fear. He asked me what I feared most, and immediately I said I did not want to hear this part. But I let it come anyway. What I heard is that there is something in particular that has to do with the beadle in the witch lifetime that is like a climax of a certain pattern. It's like a twist, like a turn of the knife that is meant to get you so that you can't move in any direction. I get the weirdest imagery! I hear the words, "It has to do with Darkness cloaked in love." I heard You say that if I understood the dynamics of the story with the beadle, I would begin to understand what feels so stuck in me from a much deeper perspective. I didn't want to hear it. I did not want to see it. And yet I couldn't *not* see it.

I love the beadle, but I am not married to him. I am married to someone else. I love the beadle and he loves me. He is, of course, a man of the church and when I am accused of heresy, he is terribly frightened. He begs me not to tell anyone about us. I am naïve. I would never expose him, but I am in agonizing disbelief when he does nothing to save me. They say I'm a heretic because I told people Jesus came to me. But I'm so afraid it's really about infidelity. Am I a sinner after all? I'm hurting so many people. There's nothing I can say, no way to defend myself. Terror. I'm crazy. It's my own fault. I thought I opened my heart to Jesus, but look what I've done. Why won't he help me? Why won't any of them help me?

And so I die with all the judgment of others — their hatred, rage, rejection and fear of me — still attached to me. I die a hideous lonely death. AND I die believing that my truth will literally kill me and hurt everyone I love.

This was all very difficult for me to take in. I have loved my father in this life and have felt a definite need to protect him. I did not want to hear anything threatening to my present-day love for him, even if it was from another lifetime. And yet everything that was told to me, even on the subtlest emotional levels, rang absolutely true. Could it be that very dark energy came to me in this lifetime not only from my own past life experience but from past life energies attached to other people? Is this part of the nature of a negative entity? Could it be that I can see people here in my present life but in some way inaccessible to my conscious mind also remember them from the past, and *feel* them from the past? Am I still subject to the energies they carry from the past just as I am subject to my own? Could there actually be a carry-over from a past life of loving my father deeply but also feeling a need to protect him, even if he didn't protect me? And was there more?

You said to me, *Negative entities play with and activate ego energies. Soul Guides (some of Us) are what you might describe as condensations of Soul energy or specific condensations of the energy of Oneness. Our presence activates, stimulates and enhances Soul consciousness in form. What you call negative entities are dense condensations of certain ego energies that activate, stimulate and enhance the ego energies you consider destructive or hurtful.*

The projected and internalized ego energies left unresolved at the time of death do not disappear. They travel with you lifetime after lifetime just as Soul Guide energy also travels with you through lifetimes. The unresolved Dark or ego energies coalesce and act as a negative force keeping you more bound to the Horizontal Plane. AND, *for every projection that is internalized, there is a corresponding projection going out. For victims of violence who have had hatred, rejection, shame, envy, or blame projected onto them, there is, on the ego level, some corresponding ego projection going back to the perpetrators — fear, hatred, resentment, resignation, submissiveness, stoicism, detachment, desire for retaliation, etc. These are what you call defenses in your psychological world — all totally understandable and, on the ego plane, often what you would consider completely justifiable.* **Understand, however, that these corresponding projections of energy, no matter how understandable, are also part of the glue that keeps perpetrator/victim bound to one another energetically on the Horizontal Plane, AND from one lifetime to another.** *The powerful negative projections you internalized in the witch lifetime that you were unable to resolve before your death AND your own corresponding projections of fear, confusion, anger and self-blame, are literally in attendance with you in this lifetime. All this projected ego energy is what you are Undoing, "eating," and transforming at this stage of your work.*

Negative projected and internalized energies do not have to involve crime or violence. One can project envy, lust, indifference, intolerance, superiority or inferiority and it is all the same spider web of ego consciousness, though some projections feel more acceptable or more tolerable than others.

What you consider positive ego energies also attend you from past lives. These are energies attached to and emanating from those in your Soul Circle who have been supportive, affirming and loving, those who have helped you or championed your cause. These positive entities are sometimes believed to be sources of inspiration that appear in dreams. Or they are believed to be angels who break through the veil of disembodiment and appear (sometimes literally) to help at critical times.

Attending condensations of Soul energy also travel with you, just as We are in attendance with you. Soul energy configurations are not the same as attending positive ego entities and they do not appear in the same way for everyone. But they all open the door to Return or Ascension on the Vertical Plane when that time comes.

This helped me see that what we consider physical is also vibrational, and vice versa – what we consider vibrational is equally physical. In fact, the line between form and energy, between the incarnate and the dis-embodied world, became blurry. And while it was both helpful and fascinating to see my experience in this totally new way, it was also very uncomfortable.

It is the intersection of these two energies, Soul energy and ego energy – what you might call Light and Darkness – that have become the stuff of myths. Epic images of Light battling Dark come to mind. However, **WE are not doing battle with these Dark energies,** *which is what your mythology is all about.* **True Light does not do battle with Darkness. Light illuminates and in that illumination, Darkness disappears. This is why all so-called religion that fights what it calls evil or non-belief with war and persecution, shame and hatred, emotional coercion or moral superiority, even on the subtlest levels, carries no Light whatsoever in Our sense of Light.**

You see, there is no real Evil; **there is only ignorance of the Plan.** *What We do here with you is light up the ignorance in which you have lived so that it disappears and the Light of the Plan is revealed.*

I loved every word, and yet I felt like I was attacking the "church," a church I have had absolutely no relationship with or even interest in, in this lifetime. But Their words had become my words, and so the fear generated in me by Their views of much of religion struck deep into that place that was surely a carry-over from past lives. Without any conscious intent on my part at all, I seemed to have entered yet another lifetime in which I would speak something that would surely be very threatening to established religion! The fear of heresy was visceral. While I loved everything They said about Jesus, at the same time, I was shocked and frightened that They made such precise references to him and spoke in Christian terms. Talking about Jesus had gotten me killed in my witch life. In this life, Soul was guiding me to talk about Jesus yet again, imbuing me with an alternative view of who he was that once again felt like it put me at risk. AND, at the same time, I could feel the very Dark energies from my witch lifetime trying to silence me, energies from outside me and energies I had internalized. Everything They said fit.

As for the Plan, They seemed to be saying that the journey we have undertaken from the Sleep of Forgetting to awakening into Soul consciousness — the journey itself is part of a Plan and that as we awaken, the Plan is further revealed. *And*, that They are a voice of that Revelation.

Sometimes you feel you have to choose between Us and some aspect of daily living, that you cannot be in both spaces at once. This is also an imprint from the past life We showed you. You could not, in that life and in many other lives, express your inner world safely in your outer world, and the shadow of this darkness is what generates so much fear in the present. You died believing that the personality could not safely house the Soul or show it in the outer world and so you came into this life prepared to shut off access to Soul on the ego level.

BUT, you also came in with the intention to bring Soul safely into the light of day this time around. In the process of that emergence, you have the conflicting experience over and over again of wanting to cling to some perceived safety in hiding while also wanting to speak. And the part that wants to bring Soul into the light of day, which you might say is Soul itself, has to keep "calling you Home." This is why you have to distinguish and

Undo the Dark ego energies attending you from the past as well as the present — because they all act together to push you back into hiding. **Soul inevitably, for you and for everyone, at some time brings you face to face with all the dense ego energies that have kept you from experiencing your true Soul nature.**

Personality, with the valve to Soul shut off, is a dry husk, especially for anyone who is at a place of retracting so much energy from the Horizontal Plane. When you move into the Great Circle of Undoing — Undoing the trances of ego that have kept you bound to the Horizontal Plane– the personality may begin to feel lost. This is not, however, bad. This is what personality feels when you begin to assume more of your vehicle nature. Its power dwindles. Bow to this. Don't criticize the personality for doing what personalities do.

Right now, you are working to Undo the power of your belief in all the negative energies you have absorbed and projected. Remember what we told you about Supreme Surrender. You **consume** *all ego-based energies within and without. You burn them at the base of the spine, breathe the Fire energy that is released up and around the Cross, breathe in Soul Light and Love and breathe it out across the Horizontal Plane.*

Chapter 20

My Daughter and My Soul Circle

And so, there was no escaping it. I might not have been tied to a stake or thrown into an oven in this life, but My Soul was asking me to stand in the Fires of loneliness, "heresy," and my daughter's drug addiction over and over again – to stand on my Cross *willingly* and keep breathing with God. It was beyond difficult.

Izzi came home for her friend Joan's sister's wedding. (Joan was the girl Izzi first got into drugs with.) I don't trust her at all. I had a bad feeling about Izzi staying with her and I said so. But Izzi is no longer a child and I can't tell her what to do.

At 11:00 pm Joan called me. She said Izzi took two Clonopin and is asleep on the couch. She said Izzi hasn't been sober at all, that she took six Clonopin and some alcohol last night and that Joan had to hide the Clonopin and have a major confrontation with Izzi to keep her from drinking. She said Izzi is trying to figure out a way to steal money off my credit card.

I knew it was bad, but I really had no idea it was this bad. I believed Izzi when she said she quit drinking. She defended herself yesterday morning against my concerns about her slurred speech with the same old insistence and righteous indignation I know so well.

Even so, her fury still frightens and overwhelms me. I don't know if I can feel yet all the pain of this. Ridiculous as it is, I still fall into that place where I want to believe she is okay.

After I got off the phone, I asked You to be with me and to tell me what I needed to do on the Soul side of this. You said very clearly that I need to walk through this Fire, carry this Cross, with my head up, without blaming myself or condemning myself or hating myself. You reminded me of what You said about Christ not hating himself on the Cross and You said that is the same position I am asked to take. I did the meditation before I went to bed and I said the prayer several times, really trying with all my might to listen to every word. Then I woke up around 3:00 a.m. nauseous and with too much anxiety to sleep.

*You are in a Fire, a big one, and you are agreeing to walk through it. We are here to help you and support you. You remembered something last night that We want to bring back for you. At the stake, at the final moment, when you looked at the child who was burned along with you, you closed your eyes. You let go of her eyes that were locked into yours. You could not bear the pain. There is a wish to close your eyes that has followed you into this life in regard to the pain of your children in particular. It is connected to the depths of despair at your utter helplessness and the added torture of witnessing the un-witnessable – for you see, **she was YOUR daughter. And her father was the beadle.***

The last big piece of that puzzle snapped into place... A long sigh of recognition echoed through my heart. The little girl who died with me was *my daughter*, and her father abandoned her as well as me. I could protect no one, save no one, and I couldn't bear to see. And now here I faced the possible death of my daughter in this life, and even though Izzi was not the daughter who died along with me in the past life, the dynamic was the same. I couldn't bear to see the full extent of the pain and destruction. I felt helpless, I believed it was all my fault. I kept closing my eyes. Opening them meant standing on a Cross I didn't believe I had the strength to stand on, and yet here in this life there was no choice.

Do not criticize yourself. This is a deep imprint filled with the fear of agonizing death. Simply know this now and let it go. There is no blame. It is old material to be Redeemed, not relived in the present.

This is the Way of Christ, the Redeemer. The act of Redemption is the act of participating consciously and with Love in every step of your chosen Path that in past lifetimes you resisted or feared or devalued or avoided. This is another way to define Supreme Surrender. There is no mystery, you see? What is on your plate now, in essence, is what has always been on your plate since the beginning of your Circle of Incarnations, in whatever variety of forms you have chosen and been assigned. This is why the reading of past lives is really nothing terribly esoteric, once you begin to understand the basic principles of incarnation and the meaning of individual events and patterns within the larger whole.

Open your eyes. You can do it. The Fire that once burned you will now Redeem you. There is only God everywhere.

I'm trying. I really am.

As a Soul moves through its incarnations, it always takes with it the Souls who have agreed to carry the corresponding parts in the Play. In other words, the one persecuted always has the Souls of the persecutors in attendance. It always has the Souls of its allies in attendance, the Souls of the witnesses, and so on. For example, the Souls of those who make great scientific breakthroughs always carry in attendance those who support them and those who doubt or deny or fight their findings or seek to block the implementation of their discoveries. You all agree to travel your road together

from the beginning. *Therefore, your parents' attachment to you and you to them is inherent in your Soul Circle. Your daughter's attachment to you and you to her is inherent in your Soul Circle.*

> Can you say more to me about Izzi? I am so worried about her and I also feel that at least a part of her wants to get better. The things You said did help. But alongside whatever perspective I have, I also have my intense emotions.

Everything is Teacher. Part of the reason why you have the intense feelings you do at this time is because your daughter needs to receive that type of transmission, that kind of intense caring and involvement. She needs emotional input, needs very much to feel certain feelings from the outside that she has difficulty generating from the inside.

Your reactions will be the most charged, most dense, and most triggering with all those you travel most closely with on your journey through lifetimes – with your daughter, your parents, Bill– and this is as it should be. This is the Sand you have asked to transform into Pearls.

The work of Undoing involves slowing down the vibration of your own energy in relation to others, shifting from an ego vibration to a Soul vibration. *This is why certain meditation practices are helpful – the vibration rate of energy is slowed and you are able to open to different levels of consciousness. You notice that Our presence brings a different vibration into your body and your psyche than you ordinarily experience. Often the closer someone is to you in your Circle of Incarnations, the more effort is required to slow the vibration down. But at the same time, there is more energy available to be released and Redeemed for use by Soul in these relationships. You can become aware of your own participation in the psychic lives of others, and your daughter's life in particular, through specifically visualizing and learning to regulate the vibrations that you receive and emit.*

The more a person begins to leave the strictly ego aspects of experience, the more they become free from the automatic action/reaction force of Gravity, the slower their vibrations become, the less dense the atmosphere around them, and the clearer their "vision" becomes. You see, there is always a molecular, material, energetic explanation or configuration that may be understood, described and perceived that attends any phenomena of the manifest world. We help slow this vibration down for you and this automatically opens your vision. You will learn to do this for yourself.

*With your daughter, remember that there is far more Soul intent behind this simultaneous incarnation than either of you could yet possibly fathom. It is so very important that you understand that for you now, **spiritual growth does not mean leaving the ego or the Horizontal Plane as your arena of participation**. You continue to live and function in your manifest world, but you leave the Horizontal Plane internally in terms of no longer operating yourself according to the laws of that plane. **You do not leave the ego plane environment**. You use it, love it, surrender the energies it holds for you and Redeem them.*

Therefore, in terms of your daughter, the depth of the mother-daughter bond provides a powerful opportunity. She needs and requires exactly what you have to give her. You must not feel that because you became highly emotional with her that you failed. She actually does not need and would not profit from your staying in some imagined calm, composed state. Now this is a tricky spot on the Road of Return. Too often people mistakenly believe that the more advanced they are in their spiritual work, the more calm control they have over their behavior and the more "detached" they are supposed to become from the Horizontal Plane. While it is true in essence that progress on the Path does away with certain unconscious reactive states, the tendency of seekers to construct an internal picture of what this looks like is often terribly premature and immature, reflecting unresolved psychological issues rather than anything particularly spiritual. This premature detachment might arise from fear of involvement, feelings of superiority or inferiority, fears of being assertive or committed, fear of taking a stand, fear of failure, or from the misguided belief that spirituality means detaching from ordinary life altogether. **The goal is not psychological or emotional detachment — it is active Participation as a Soul.**

Surrender is the ultimate place of appropriate inner control and composure *from Our point of view. You Surrender to all known Circles of Being in which you exist together with all beings. On the level that you are the animal mother of your daughter, your mothering impulses toward her are an inevitable and agreed upon part of the relationship, no matter what the issue or situation. You embrace your primal instincts to protect your daughter's body and her being from harm. That is one level. On another level, you Surrender to all aspects of the parts you play for each other in your personal Circle of Incarnations. You surrender to all the ways she is Teacher for you.*

Your feelings and concerns are appropriate. None of your responses are supposed to be sublimated. You are not supposed to rise above them as you progress. They are to be understood and worked with. How do you Surrender the pain, distress, fear, confusion, and uncertainty of your ordinary life circumstances and relationships — how do you Surrender all that to be transformed for use by Soul and God, **while remaining intimately involved** *on an ordinary level? This, you could say, is the first big challenge on the Road Home. And the Path of Supreme Surrender is your guide.*

Understand that the glue of the parent/child bond is not the same as the pull of Gravity. The attachment inherent in family bonds is a manifestation of Soul adaptation to form in humans. It is part of your innate survival instinct. When your baby is in danger, you are not acting out of an ego impulse when you snatch her from the jaws of a lion. Do you see how you do not want to confuse these impulses?

Now, at the level where you begin to grasp that you incarnated as her mother and she as your daughter for a Soul purpose, you will either be working in a context of Karma creation or Karma

Undoing. In the work of Undoing Gravity, on the Road of Return, **Surrender means that you see her as Teacher, first and foremost, but that does NOT mean you weaken or pull back from involvement.** *It does not mean you tell yourself she has her own Karmic Path and therefore you leave her to God and her own devices. It means that you surrender to Teacher in all interactions with her,* **Teacher for you.**

What did I come to learn from my relationship with my daughter? How could I stay intimately involved with her (how could I not?) and Surrender, accept all that is, at the same time? As I did the Breath of the Cross Meditation, as I haltingly "chose" to stand in that Fire, one thing was becoming clear. I was learning to have my voice regardless of the response. My mother instinct called me to keep speaking out despite her angry resistance. And my Soul called me to the very same thing—speak your truth. Speak anyway. Your truth and your life force and your Soul are all connected. This was a repeating theme. Lifetimes of fear and brutal silencing would be thrown into that Fire to be Redeemed. Of course that Fire was hot! But They would show me the way. I see now that Teacher in each of us will point the way to the learning we each came into body to make conscious for ourselves and for our fellow human beings. Back then it took everything I had to keep turning to the Teacher that came in the form of my daughter's life-threatening drug addiction. It took everything I had not to be consumed in those flames.

You must judge nothing and predetermine nothing. Nuclear family and family of origin relationships are powerful Teachers because the Karmic or ego bonds in those relationships are so tight, the energies so dense. Those relationships can provide the greatest learning. You can learn good parenting techniques and how to deal with an addicted family member from a book and from others. That is all well and good, appropriate and very needed. But when you Surrender the energies held in a tight Karmic bond to Soul, you then take direction from your own Soul as to what **your Soul Path** *is at the juncture where your two energies meet. You learn from the very act of Surrender itself. One person's Soul direction may be to have a more powerful voice, another's to love more deeply, find their wisdom, become more creative, address stuck religious beliefs, or let go altogether. No one really knows but you.*

In addition, you will learn to look at family relationships, but really all relationships, from the standpoint of where you meet others in what We call the Circle of Social Evolution. **Each person's difficulties, challenges, and greatest gifts call to specific issues facing the entire human race. They exemplify specific themes in the great Play of human consciousness.** *As you learn to see and understand your role in playing out these world themes, the meaning and purpose of your relationships and issues are greatly expanded. You begin to see that you are each part of the evolution of human consciousness in a collective and not just a personal sense. We will say much more about this later. For now, understand that it doesn't matter if the scale on which these issues are being played out is what you consider a large scale or a small scale. We are not talking about numbers of people or spheres of influence – those are ego judgments. We are talking about energies. In the Circle of Social Evolution, Izzi calls to issues of disconnection from the feminine and a skewed use of the masculine, resulting in self-harm and addiction, and therefore, in her Soul, she calls loudly to the reunification of the Masculine/Feminine Duality. In the Circle of Social Evolution, you call to the issues of a silenced voice, and the disconnection from self and other that is the result.*

*You see, too, why you became a psychotherapist – your Soul is calling you to heal the injury of disconnection from self and other through wise communication. Each person can begin to understand himself and his relationships from the point of view of the Circle of Social Evolution in this way – what **you are trying to heal in yourself, you are trying to heal for humanity**. And the converse is also true – **what you are not trying to heal in yourself, you perpetuate as Karma for humanity**. This is not a statement of threat or blame. It is lawful that Karma is* *perpetuated until one enters the Road of Return. As a personality, you may not like the role another has played in your life. They may have hurt you, betrayed you, ignored you or abandoned you.* **But as a Soul, each in his own way, from whatever level of consciousness he operates on, is calling YOU to heal some unintegrated, underdeveloped, or lost part of yourself and of the Race of Man. THIS is the most healing approach to human relations. This is how you see Teacher in all beings and all circumstances.**

When you Surrender to these roles and lines of mutual impact on each other with conscious awareness of what you are doing, as opposed to resisting your differences or trying to force change on the other, you participate with them in using the very Sand which was given to you to make the transition from the Horizontal to the Vertical Plane.

Surrender means you learn how to welcome the abrasiveness of these personal challenges, you use the friction of that abrasiveness to fire the engines of your own transformation—not theirs—because it is in transforming yourself that you contribute to the illumination of Soul on Earth for everyone. This is what it means to make Pearls from Sand. Pearls are the concrete manifestation of Redemption in your world. If you run from the Sand or try only to smooth its edges, you lose this opportunity. Ego tries to run from, alter or destroy that abrasiveness, often with force. Soul embraces, enlivens and transforms it through Love.

Reading over this material from my journal I am struck over and over again by the global significance and power of these words. It is glaringly obvious, in this time of instantaneous worldwide communication and the intricately interwoven dependencies between all people everywhere, that my Soul Circle, the group of mutually incarnating Souls I travel with, IS NOW EVERYONE. We are, whether we can always see it or not, dependent on millions of people we will never know or ever meet, but whose beliefs and actions can change our own lives in an instant. The close and highly impactful relationships I had back in the 90's and have now in 2017, the people in my immediate family and my close friends, are some of the central players in my brief act in my little scene in a play that is truly global in nature in a way that has never been visible before. We may have always been in that Play together with the entire human race, but today we know it even if we don't want to take it in.

I am awed by the fact that the dense ego energies which are bombarding us and which we are called to transform, are the ego energies *of the entire human race*, not just the energies that are playing out in our small immediate Circles—which, by the way, are plenty intense all by themselves. The daily minute-by-minute blast of projected ego energy, of worldwide judgment of right and wrong, good and evil, have and have not, love and hate, pleasure and pain, creation and destruction, and domination and submission, is at a fever pitch.

I am awed by the fact that some of my greatest Teachers have been the people and circumstances that appeared to cause me the greatest pain, and that the greatest good did come from the Fires I was asked and "chose" to stand in. In today's world, the challenge to see Teacher in many of the players front and center on the world stage, the challenge to stand in the Fire of so many threats to our continued existence—*and not be burned, but keep my eyes open and focused on the Light of Soul Pushing Through to consciousness*—for me, that challenge has never been greater.

*There is not one among you who is not equal to the task. The difficulty comes in fully understanding what exactly that task is. Try becoming aware, alongside your animal, mother, therapist, intelligent, socially refined responses to your daughter, of the Divine playing out through her **exactly as she is**. This is what*

*We call a Soul response that you **include** with the other responses you are of course more accustomed to. **Not to replace** all the other responses with what We call the Soul response– that is the challenge We referred to above. Too many people too often attempt to leave the ego plane too soon. The intricacies and difficulties as well as the joys and fulfilling aspects of your relationships with anyone and everyone are your food, her food, and everyone's food. They are the yolk of your egg. You eat it all in order to grow your wings and fly.*

*What does this mean? You are Izzi's mother. You instinctively want her to be safe, to thrive, to find happiness, fulfillment and love. You foster whatever you as her mother can foster in order to help her move in the directions you believe are valuable. That is the role you incarnated into with her, and she asked for that role by incarnating as your daughter. **You can meet the obstacles to fulfilling your role with either the full force of your personality or the full force of your Soul.***

*As you move into the center of the Cross, you learn to transform the personality response – **which will lawfully continue to be there** – into Soul consciousness. You take the pain or the frustration or fear you feel with your daughter – whatever you feel with her – and you breathe it through the Cross inside you, and you give all the energy tightly bound in your Karmic relationship with her to your Soul. You fill your heart with Divine Love and then you breathe that energy back out into the world and into your relationship with your daughter. You begin to understand that she brought you very specific challenges in the awakening of your voice – that in the face of her anger, resistance, defiance and pain, you are challenged to speak anyway, hold to your truth anyway, love her as a Soul anyway, and continue to see and speak to Soul in her anyway, no matter what her personality is manifesting on the Horizontal Plane. **You are forging your own Soul consciousness out of this Sand. This is the essence of Surrender, the essence of Redemption. This is Pearl.***

I don't know that I can ever convey the depth of a Love not of this Earth that I felt in those words, and a Wisdom of acceptance outside any judgment at all. The pain and shame and powerlessness I carried about my daughter's addiction, about the severity of her "failure to thrive" in the nest that *I* had provided for her, had a whole new meaning and purpose in the light God brought to my suffering and fear. They helped me begin to see all of human life through this much larger lens. My pain as her mother might not have been less, but there was meaning, there was purpose, and there was something in my own heart and Soul I could actually do.

The concept of the Circle of Social Evolution was fascinating. The idea that together we all play specific parts in the unfolding of the evolution of human consciousness and that our individual parts are all strands of a much larger fabric that is REAL and has purpose and direction, greatly expanded my respect and compassion for our personal trials within this complex human drama. Someone like myself whose throat had been so constricted, who found it so difficult to speak or connect to others, and who could barely nurture herself in so many basic ways — someone like me who was relatively no one in the grand scheme of things by ego's evaluation, was actually playing out world themes of silence by force and of disconnection from self, other, and Soul through denial of my own truths.

I was being called upon, by my daughter's extreme self-destructive behavior, to find my voice, to hold the lifeline of connection and to nurture us both. I was being called upon by the very real threat of her overdosing, to activate not only my feminine receptive but also my masculine assertive energies and *do something,* and the main avenue I had with her was always through speaking my truth.

The terror of the situation was calling me to heal, to grow in the deepest sense of the word I had ever known. It would be slow going on a very long road. My own disconnection very early in life had left me paralyzed in so many ways.

My daughter was calling me to re-awaken my mother instinct to protect my young. What? Wasn't I born with that? Well, I'm sure I was, but whatever happened to me early on left me, for the most part, unable to protect *myself*, and that carried over to an inability to protect my children in ways that are still very painful to recall. To say nothing of the leftovers from the witch life.

When I was a junior in college I went with my boyfriend to a party where people were doing drugs. Although it was the late 60's, I was so naïve and inexperienced I didn't have a clue. I remember being appalled that the woman who answered the door was completely naked, but it never occurred to me to say I wanted to leave. I was like a spectator to the play of my life—like it was all unfolding on a stage around me, like I had no part in writing the script and I couldn't change any scene or exit the stage.

There was a young couple with an infant at the party. Suddenly, the father picked up his baby and threatened to throw it against the wall. There was a huge commotion. I don't remember being a part of it. I was completely paralyzed. Someone must have stopped this drug-crazed man and called the police, but everything after that moment is a blur, like when your TV loses reception and you miss an entire segment of a show. Suddenly I found myself out in the hallway and everyone was gone and my boyfriend was mad at me but I had no idea why and I had no idea what happened.

The only thing that is *not* a blur is the memory of paralysis. Everything was frozen inside me—the masculine, the feminine, the voice I needed in order to find them both and the physical body that housed it all.

Many years later, when I had my first child, Eddie, there was a glimmer of awakening. I had just come home from the hospital and my parents were visiting. I had nursed Eddie and put him down in his little basket bed. My mother and I were sitting at the kitchen table when Eddie began to cry. I got up to go to him. My mother immediately said, "Leave him alone. They have to cry it out. It's good for their lungs." Paralysis. I wanted to go to him. My mother said no. I wanted to go to him but I couldn't move my body under the weight of her injunction. There was a war going on in my psyche. It was an absolutely pivotal moment. Finally, I went to my baby and picked him up. One small step in breaking a powerful trance. Sadly, it took me many, many years before I could respond appropriately to other kinds of cries.

Now let me tell you one more story. Early on in my writing, They showed me a past life in which Izzi and I were both men working on a ship. The man she was, was accused of committing a crime and sentenced to walk the plank. He did not try to save himself. He was bound with heavy rope from his shoulders down past his hands and he was glaringly defiant until the end. Not being able to do anything else, I offered him a drink of water but he refused, spat in the face of his accusers and went to his death. As you might remember, I was also shown that Izzi was my youngest daughter in the witch life and that she was about three when I died. So, I saw two lives of extreme helplessness in relation to her. In both lives I couldn't help her, and in the witch life she also couldn't help me.

There is a beautiful irony, or perhaps further evidence of the possibility of Redemption in human relationships, in the fact that in this present life we have both been on the edge of extinction in very different ways, and our roles as mother and daughter have given us both the most unforeseen opportunity to come back from the edge and live.

If I had not been given this extraordinary gift of the writing, if I had not been able to see our present day relationship through anything other than a conventional lens, I would have been completely lost in self-judgment—not a good mother, co-dependent, my fault that my baby was an addict, that she was killing herself, what kind of a therapist are you, how can you help other people if you can't even help your own child, if you let this happen? I would have been lost in fear. Not that I wasn't often lost in fear and judgment. I was. Not that there isn't a place for self-reflection, accountability, and even diagnosis—certainly there is.

But unerringly, They lifted me up out of that Horizontal Plane perspective and gave me the Soul's eye view of what we really came here, in exactly these forms in exactly these roles and extreme challenges, to transform and Redeem. In my precious moments of connection to Them, I was lifted out of the place of **all judgment**. And for me, that is the doorway God opens, the doorway out of the old Garden of Eden and all the Good and Evil seeds that were sown there.

So you see, in this most difficult of intersections with my daughter, They took the shame out of all that apparent failure and transformed our story into a healing journey. We might have been at the start of a very long road, but we were both being called to great transformation—IF we could look at it that way.

Back in the 90's, it was terribly difficult for me to stay at that level of consciousness for more than a few moments at a time. For the most part, I could barely keep my head above water and was unable to think about world themes or our places in the Circle of Social Evolution. I was just desperate to find my next breath and a life jacket for my daughter. But looking back now, I know how hard I held onto that life-line, both to Them and to her, and I can never express the gratitude I have for how They stayed with me every step of the way, how the moments when I was able to come up for air were filled with Their Divine Love, Understanding and Light beyond measure.

Here in 2017, as I watch the Play unfolding on the world stage, the Terror of the Situation for me is no longer purely personal the way it was back in the 90's. Are we, as a race of beings, already throwing the baby against the wall? I do not want to repeat my old pattern of paralysis, of silence in the face of overwhelming threat. I want to have the faith to hear the voice of Teacher everywhere, to have my voice no matter what. I know I am not alone. Countless Souls are responding to the evolutionary call to shift our consciousness now **in order to survive**.

I know now that we are ALL being called to great transformation — IF we can see it that way.

Open your eyes. You can do it. The Fire that once burned you will now Redeem you. There is only God everywhere.

Afterword

nce again, there is no perfect place to end this book. The journey continued and the flow of Divine Love, Wisdom, direction and perspective kept expanding. In the books to come, I will share with you all that I was taught about the chakra energies and how to use them in the **Breath of the Cross Meditation,** how to use that chakra information to further illuminate your own personal Soul Path, and how to understand your personal Soul Path as your access to Service and participation in Planetary Return.

About the Author

*P*hyllis Leavitt started writing poetry when she was thirteen and later wrote and illustrated many children's books. In her early twenties, she embarked on a spiritual journey. She didn't go on a pilgrimage to the Far East or sit long hours in meditation, and though she tried many spiritual paths, she always returned to writing as her prayer and her practice. One early poem was entitled "My God is This Empty Sheet of Paper."

Phyllis could not have known back then how prophetic that poem title would be. But finally, in 1995, while she was journaling her way through the very darkest time of her life, her writing took a dramatic turn.

A Divine Voice spoke to her as she wrote page after page about her painful wanderings through the dark mystery of her childhood and the wilderness of her adult life. Though she had worshiped for as long as she could remember at the feet of that great God "Writing," she could not have known that God and Soul would hear her prayers and literally fill that empty sheet of paper. Suddenly God was right there talking to her about what her Soul was seeking within all the life experiences of Phyllis Leavitt, and especially in all that she found so difficult.

"They" spoke volumes. She wrote down all the messages given to her from early 1995 to 1998 but eventually, overcome by tremendous self-doubt, she put it all away. Then one day in 2011, when her husband was in great pain from a surgery and questioning the whole experience of being in a body, she suddenly found herself talking to him about her writing, about the Soul purpose in all our experience, about all pain being Soul calling us Home. Her Soul was calling her Home through that experience with her husband. From there it was only a matter of time before she decided to write her book.

***

Phyllis Leavitt has a Master's Degree in Psychology and Counseling and has been in private practice for over 25 years. She is the author of *The Road Home: A Light in the Darkness*, Book I of **The Road Home Series**, soon to be re-issued under the title, *A Light in the Darkness*. *Into the Fire* is Book II in that series. She has given several public talks on her work and co-hosts the "Light on the Road Home" podcast with Deborah Louise Brown (blogtalkradio.com/boomerandbabe).

Phyllis lives with her husband in Santa Fe and Taos, New Mexico. She is passionate about nature, hiking, camping, and being with her children and grandchildren. She also enjoys painting; the front and back covers of her books feature her paintings.

Visit her website at PhyllisLeavitt.com or contact her at phyllisleavitt@phyllisleavitt.com

Definitions of Terms

Here are definitions of the terms that are central to the concepts that emerge in the communication from the Divine Voice that spoke to me. The list is not in alphabetical order to follow a flow of the natural association of these ideas.

Spiritual Work — True spiritual work is active participation in the evolution of human consciousness.

Map of the Road Home — The blueprint of the journey from ego consciousness to Soul consciousness.

Horizontal Plane — Ego consciousness, the state of separation, a consciousness in which we project our beliefs, feelings, ideas and impulses onto others and internalize those same projections from others; the arena of action/reaction in which we bounce back and forth between the two sides of all Dualities — Good/Evil, Right/Wrong, Domination/Submission, Have/Have Not, Pleasure/Pain, Masculine/Feminine, etc. — and in which we are subject to all the laws keeping us unaware of our Soul nature.

Vertical Plane — The plane of consciousness that is entered as we become aware of our Soul nature and begin the ever expanding and deepening process of lighting up Soul consciousness within us on the Road of Return to Oneness.

Undoing—The process of freeing ourselves from all that has kept us in ego consciousness. The process of giving back all projected ego energies taken on and internalized over the course of our incarnations. The process of understanding and taking apart the patterns of our Karmic path in order to allow the light of Soul to be expressed though our incarnated forms.

Revelation—The illumination of the structures, laws and dynamics that have both created our ego consciousness AND provide us with the road map of Return to Soul consciousness and Oneness; illumination of how all that which has become separate in consciousness is reunited: the understanding of *oneself as the Way,* of one's place in the universe on every level.

Redemption—The process by which energy is released from ego consciousness, "burned up," and the pure energy released from that Fire is then available for use by Soul; the energetic process of moving from the Horizontal Plane to the Vertical Plane.

Supreme Surrender—Surrender to What Is; a heart response to the call of Soul within us that supersedes the pull of the personality; the specific process by which ego energy is made available for Soul's expression in the world through our human forms.

Laws of Gravity—The laws that created the original state of separation, the Sleep of Forgetting the Source. The laws that determine the lens through which ego consciousness perceives and responds to the world of self and other that keep us separate; the forces that keep our awareness on the Horizontal Plane and unaware of our Soul essence.

Karma — Another word for ego consciousness and the dense ego energies accumulated over lifetimes from patterns of action and reaction on the Horizontal Plane; that which is Undone on the Road of Return; NOT a law of retribution. The friction of opposites (Duality) and all the possible projected ego energies that arise from it make up the Karmic level of existence. This friction of opposites is also the Food that is eaten in the process of Return.

Soul Seed — The Soul Seed of the individual contains the entire "map" of their path through all their incarnations and their journey through ego consciousness, *as well as* the map of their particular Path of Return to Oneness.

The Play — In ego consciousness, we keep projecting our thoughts, feelings, actions and energies — lawfully — out onto the Horizontal Plane according to the part in the Play each of us was asked and agreed to play. These parts invoke the reactive responses of others that make up the Play we create together. We each play a part in the creation of Karma and we each play a part on the Path of Return in which we make a specific contribution to the illumination of Soul for us all.

Fire — The principle of burning up ego consciousness to release pure energy for use by Soul on the Road of Return to Oneness.

The Cross — Formed by the intersection of the Horizontal and Vertical Planes. The heart lies at the center of the Cross and it is the entry point into the Road of Return. The Cross can also be understood as the challenges, themes, obstacles, etc., we carry through our ego existence until we *stand* on that same Cross as Jesus did, offering ourselves to be of Service for the Return of All to Oneness.

Teacher—The principle of seeing all states of being, all relationships, people, events, circumstances, attractions and repulsions as exactly what we came here, as Souls, to *learn from,* rather than judge, avoid, deny, hate or idolize, in the process of Undoing Karma. That which shows us where *we* (not others) are blocked from receiving and transmitting Divine Love through our incarnate form.

The Holy Ghost— All that we interact with on the Horizontal Plane—people, ideas, physical conditions, political movements, food production, wealth distribution, disease, religion, all the other kingdoms of the planet Earth, the cosmos around us—*everything* outside us that we interact with and which interacts with us.

The Shadow of the Holy Ghost— What we consider the Dark side of all that we interact with, internally and externally. This is the Darkness that human beings believe is a part of themselves. The Shadow of the Holy Ghost is **projected ego energy** which has been internalized, believed, and acted out on the Horizontal Plane, which then further tightens and strengthens the web of projected energies in which human beings solidify their beliefs about themselves and determine what strategies they will use to survive.

Soul Parts— All the unresolved aspects of past life experiences that we carry with us into our present lives. What we call the inner child is the core essence of all our Soul Parts. It is the psychic embodiment of the unconscious aspects of all previous incarnations.

Soul Circle—Those Souls that travel most closely with us through lifetimes, offering the energies and experiences needed in the development and proliferation of ego consciousness *and* offering the energies and experiences asked for on the Road of Return to Oneness.

Circle of Incarnations — All the incarnations a person has in human form; our "selves" in a much larger sense.

Circle of Social Evolution — The roles of individual human beings coming together to create the themes the entire human race is both developing and working with in ego consciousness *and* illuminating on the Road Home. Like the parts in a play that come together to create the overall story line, unfolding scenes, and the climax, in which everyone's individual part is essential to the whole drama.

Evolution — The process of change and development that occurs in a life form when it meets an overwhelming obstacle to survival that *necessitates* adaptation and change if that life form is to continue.

Evolution of Soul Consciousness — The use of ego consciousness as the raw material out of which Soul consciousness is created in humans. As ego consciousness itself creates the obstacles to our continued survival, the evolution of Soul consciousness becomes the adaptation most needed for our continued existence.

Sand — The principle of Resistance central to the evolution of consciousness: the irritation inside our psyches that becomes motivation to evolve consciousness from an ego state of being to a Soul state of Being. The irritation created by our very ego nature itself that ultimately drives us to create "Pearls" of Soul consciousness.

Pearl — The symbol of Soul consciousness in human beings. Just as an oyster creates pearls from coating the irritation of a grain of sand inside its shell, so we learn to transform the irritation cause by ego consciousness into Pearls of Soul Consciousness. We learn to transform human pain into Divine Love and use the finite as a bridge to the infinite.

The Sleep of Forgetting—The original trance that put the human race under the spell of ego consciousness in which we came to believe in our separateness from each other and from God, symbolized by the story of Adam and Eve.

Serpent Power—The symbolic representation of the power that put the human race under the spell of ego consciousness *and* the power that wakes us up to remembering our true Soul nature and initiates us onto the Road of Return to Oneness.

www.ingramcontent.com/pod-product-compliance
Lightning Source LLC
Chambersburg PA
CBHW051955090426
42741CB00008B/1408